NAVIGATING LIFE'S STORMS

FINDING CALM IN THE CHAOS

RAE A. STONEHOUSE

Live For Excellence Productions

NAVIGATING LIFE'S STORMS: FINDING CALM IN THE CHAOS

LIFE CAN THROW us some real curveballs sometimes. It's like we're all trying to navigate life's storms, trying to find that calm in the chaos. I've had my fair share of those storms – unexpected challenges and setbacks that seemed overwhelming. But I've learned something important: these storms, as wild as they are, can actually be opportunities for growth, if we tackle them with the right mindset.

I used to think I could steer through every storm if I planned enough. Ha! How wrong I was. No matter how smooth the sailing seems, there's always a wave waiting to rock the boat. But that's the adventure of life, isn't it? It's unpredictable, and that's just part of the deal.

The key? Learning how to ride those waves. Instead of resisting the storm or panicking when we're thrown off course, we need to become quick at adapting and see these challenges as lessons. It's not easy, I get it! But building resilience and developing strong problem-solving skills are important for navigating these uncharted waters.

And hey, you need not weather these storms alone. Having a crew – people who offer a different perspective or listen – makes a world of difference. I've learned so much from others who've braved their own storms and came out stronger. Their stories inspire me to hold on when the seas get rough.

Because believe it or not, these storms are good for us. They toughen us up, make us more adaptable, and sharpen our problem-solving skills. They push us to become the best version of ourselves, developing qualities like patience, creativity, and empathy. As hard as these experiences can be in the moment, they equip us with skills that help us long after the storm has passed.

So next time life throws you into a storm, remember it's helping you grow. Embrace the twists and turns, meet them with resilience, adaptability, and optimism. You'll likely find that you're stronger than ever once the skies clear!

I'll be sharing strategies for navigating life's storms in this book. We'll explore these topics in depth, sometimes revisiting them to gain new perspectives. My advice? Read through the entire book once, then come back to specific chapters when you need some extra guidance or a fresh outlook.

Wrapping it up, life's full of surprises, and they're here to remind us that nothing is set in stone. By being prepared, adaptable, and open to change, we can not only overcome these challenges but also come out stronger. When life throws you a curveball, remember it's setting you up for an amazing comeback. So, let's face each challenge with positivity, resilience, and a willingness to adapt, knowing these moments are shaping us into even better people.

Rae A. Stonehouse Author January 2024

COPYRIGHT

ISBN:

Ebook: 9798877854161

Paperback: 978-1-998813-60-5

Audiobook: 978-1-998813-61-2

~

SECTION ONE: THE NATURE OF UNEXPECTED CHALLENGES

INTRODUCTION TO UNEXPECTED CHALLENGES

LIFE'S LIKE A PUZZLE, isn't it? Sometimes the pieces fit neatly together, and other times, well, you get thrown a curveball that doesn't quite fit anywhere. These curveballs, or unexpected challenges as we like to call them, can knock us off our feet and test our ability to dust ourselves off and keep going. They come in all shapes and sizes – personal setbacks, professional hiccups, or just out-of-the-blue changes that make us go, "Wait, what now?" Let's break down these different types of challenges and check out some real-world examples to get a clearer picture.

Personal Setbacks: Personal setbacks are those bumps in the road that we rarely see coming, and they're usually out of our hands. Think health issues, relationship dramas, or money troubles. For instance:

- **Health Setback**: Picture a young pro who's all about their career when suddenly, they find out they have something like diabetes. They've got to flip their lifestyle upside down – changing what they eat, keeping an eye on their blood sugar, and maybe even starting new meds.

- **Relationship Setback**: Imagine a couple who's all in, planning their future together, and then boom – they hit a rough patch and break up. It's more than just heartache; it's their whole life plan thrown into a blender.
- **Financial Setback**: Think about someone who's comfortably cruising in their job, and out of nowhere, they're handed a pink slip because of budget cuts or something. Suddenly, they're crunching numbers, figuring out how to pay rent, and trying to make ends meet.

Professional Obstacles: Then there are the hurdles we jump over at work. These can be anything from tricky team members to crazy deadlines or projects that just don't pan out. Like:

- **Difficult Colleague**: Let's say you're leading a project, and there's this one team member who's always behind schedule and rubbing everyone the wrong way. It's not just annoying – it throws the whole team off their game.
- **Tight Deadline**: Imagine you're a reporter, and you've got to cover this huge story – but you've got barely any time to put together something that's not just fast, but good.
- **Failure To Achieve Desired Outcomes**: Picture an entrepreneur who's put everything into launching their dream business, but their first big marketing push is a flop. Back to the drawing board, right?

Sudden Changes in Circumstances: And then, there are those moments that come out of nowhere and turn everything upside down. Things like natural disasters, political chaos, or global emergencies. For example:

- **Natural Disaster**: Think about a family living in a hurricane-prone area. One bad storm, and they're left picking up the pieces of their home and their lives.
- **Political Unrest**: Imagine you're studying abroad, and suddenly the country you're in is hit by political turmoil.

You're stuck trying to stay safe and figure out how to get back home.

- **Global Crisis**: The COVID-19 pandemic is the perfect example of this. It hit everyone, everywhere – jobs lost, schools closed, health worries. It was a lot.

So, wrapping it up, life can throw us all kinds of curveballs. They could be personal stuff like health, relationships, or money woes, work-related issues like tough coworkers or impossible deadlines, or just big, out-of-the-blue changes like disasters or crises. Real stories like these show us just how complex and tough these challenges can be, but they also shine a light on the strength and resilience we can muster to get through them.

EMOTIONAL IMPACT OF UNEXPECTED CHALLENGES:

WHEN LIFE THROWS US A CURVEBALL, it's not just the situation that's tough, but also the whirlwind of emotions that come with it. Whether it's losing a job out of the blue, facing a health scare, or dealing with a personal problem, these challenges can stir up a whole mix of feelings – fear, frustration, uncertainty. These emotions can weigh on our minds, but the good news is, there are ways to handle them.

- **Fear**: It's usually the first thing that hits us. Fear comes from not knowing what's next and worrying about how this challenge will shake up our lives. It can make you feel stuck, anxious, even lost. The key is to face this fear head on. Know that it's okay to fear the unknown. Talking it out with friends, family, or even a professional can make a big difference. And hey, simple stuff like deep breathing or diving into a hobby can help calm those nerves too.
- **Frustration**: This one's a biggie. When we hit a roadblock, it's easy to get frustrated, especially when solutions seem out of reach. This frustration can bubble up into anger or a feeling of being powerless. It's important to be kind to yourself here. Understand that not every problem gets solved right away,

and setbacks are part of the journey. Find things that make you happy, take breaks, or let out that frustration in a healthy way, like working out or writing it down.

- **Uncertainty**: Now, this is a tricky emotion. When you're facing something unexpected, not knowing what's coming next can be unsettling. To handle this, try to focus on taking care of yourself and staying in the moment. Mindfulness practices can help lower the stress about the future. Break down the challenge into smaller, doable steps. Look for information, resources, or advice to give you stability. And lean on your support network – they're there to help you through the murky times.

Besides these strategies, keeping a positive mindset is important. Sure, it's normal to feel down during tough times, but try to look for the silver lining. Look for stories of people who've been in your shoes and made it through. Remember to be grateful for the good things in your life and celebrate even the small wins.

Emotional rollercoasters are part of dealing with life's surprises. But by acknowledging and facing our fears, being patient with our frustrations, and staying grounded during uncertainty, we can find our way through. With time, we come out on the other side stronger, wiser, and with a whole new set of skills for handling whatever life throws our way next.

OVERCOMING UNEXPECTED CHALLENGES:

So, let's talk about tackling those out-of-the-blue challenges life loves to throw at us. These moments can knock the wind out of our sails, but they're also the perfect chance to grow stronger and more capable. Being resilient, having some slick problem-solving skills, and staying flexible are superpowers when getting past these hurdles. In this chapter, we're diving into how to beef up these skills and checking out some inspiring stories of folks who've nailed it in tough times.

Cultivating Resilience: Resilience is all about bouncing back from tough spots and keeping a positive attitude. Here's how to get your resilience game strong:

- **Develop A Growth Mindset:** Look at challenges as a chance to improve. Instead of seeing failures as dead ends, think of them as lessons.
- **Practice Self-Care:** Make sure you're taking care of yourself – hit the gym, eat well, and get enough sleep. It's all about keeping your mind and body in tip-top shape.
- **Cultivate A Support Network:** Have a bunch of positive, encouraging people in your corner. They're your go-to for advice and a pep talk when things get rough.

Enhancing Problem-Solving Skills: Problem-solving is a must-have when you're faced with unexpected challenges. Here's how to sharpen those skills:

- **Seek Clarity:** Pin down exactly what the problem is, break it into smaller pieces, and tackle the most important bits first.
- **Generate Alternatives:** Brainstorm a bunch of ways to solve the problem. Think outside the box and don't be afraid to get creative.
- **Analyze And Choose:** Weigh the pros and cons of each idea, think about the risks and rewards, and then go for the option that looks best.

Embracing Flexibility: Being flexible means, you can roll with the punches and find new ways to succeed. Here are tips for staying adaptable:

- **Embrace Change:** Understand that change is just part of the game and see it as a chance to grow and try new things.
- **Foster A Growth Mindset:** Believe that every challenge is an opportunity in disguise and be open to different paths and solutions.
- **Remain Open-Minded:** Be ready to listen to other perspectives and approaches, even if they're not what you first had in mind.

Success Stories:

- **J.K. Rowling:** She got a ton of rejections before "Harry Potter" took off, but she didn't give up. Her resilience, problem-solving, and flexibility turned her story into a worldwide sensation.
- **Elon Musk:** This guy's had his fair share of setbacks (like those SpaceX rockets that kept failing), but he never stopped trying. His resilience, knack for solving problems, and ability to adapt have made SpaceX, Tesla, and his other ventures huge successes.

Conclusion: Getting over life's unexpected hiccups takes resilience, problem-solving, and the ability to adapt. By building up these skills, we can turn tough times into chances to grow and succeed. Stories of people like J.K. Rowling and Elon Musk show just how powerful these qualities can be. Remember, these challenges aren't just obstacles; they're opportunities to become stronger and achieve more than we ever thought possible.

LEARNING AND GROWTH:

STEPPING outside our comfort zones and confronting fears and limitations is often a result of facing unexpected challenges. These challenges might initially seem overwhelming, but they also have the potential to be transformative experiences that encourage personal growth and learning. The lessons we learn from such experiences are invaluable for our personal development and resilience, helping us handle future obstacles with more confidence and ease.

- **Learning Adaptability**: One of the most important lessons we get from unexpected challenges is adaptability. When faced with unforeseen obstacles, we're pushed to rethink our strategies and come up with new solutions. This process not only exposes us to different ways of thinking and possibilities but also enhances our problem-solving abilities and encourages creative thinking. It's like giving our brain a new set of tools to tackle future challenges.
- **Self-Reflection and Discovery**: Facing difficulties often leads us to introspection. When we're up against adversity, we usually examine our beliefs, values, and assumptions more closely. This introspection helps us understand ourselves

better, leading to personal growth and self-discovery. It can reveal strengths and qualities we didn't know we had, empowering us to use these newfound abilities to overcome challenges.

- **Building Resilience**: Challenges also teach us about resilience. They show setbacks and failures are not final stops, but rather steppingstones toward success. By confronting challenges directly, we develop the resilience to persist in the face of adversity. We learn to view setbacks as valuable learning opportunities, which enables us to recover more quickly and with greater determination. This resilience becomes an important trait that aids us in navigating future uncertainties confidently.
- **Fostering a Growth Mindset**: Encountering difficulties encourages us to view them as opportunities for growth rather than reasons for discouragement. We understand that failures and setbacks are not reflective of our worth or abilities but are essential parts of our growth journey. This mindset prompts us to approach challenges with curiosity and openness, continually seeking new knowledge and skills. It ignites our passion for personal development and propels us toward further growth.

Facing unexpected challenges offers a unique chance for personal growth and learning. It teaches us adaptability, self-reflection, resilience, and the importance of maintaining a growth mindset. These experiences contribute significantly to our personal development by expanding our perspectives, deepening our understanding of ourselves, and equipping us with necessary tools for future challenges. Embracing these challenges as catalysts for growth helps us cultivate resilience and the ability to thrive amidst adversity.

∼

SUPPORT AND RESOURCES:

DEALING with unexpected challenges can be tough and sometimes even feel too much. But remember, reaching out for support and making the most of the resources out there can make a huge difference. Getting this help can give you emotional backup, lighten those feelings of being all alone, and even hand you some solid advice and strategies for getting through whatever you're facing. Plus, tapping into these resources can boost your resilience and problem-solving skills, setting you up to better manage anything else that comes your way.

There's a whole bunch of support options out there for anyone dealing with a surprise challenge. Here's a quick rundown of some go-to resources:

- **Support Groups**: These are great for connecting with folks who've been in your shoes. In these groups, you can talk about what you're going through, share your experiences, and get support from people who get it. You can find these groups both in person and online.
- **Counseling Services**: Talking to a professional counselor or therapist can be helpful. They provide a private space to work

through your feelings and can guide you in developing ways to cope during tough times.

- **Online Forums and Communities**: Places like Reddit or other specialized forums are perfect for getting advice and support anonymously. These online communities can offer a bunch of viewpoints and insights, which can be valuable.
- **Helplines and Crisis Hotlines**: Many organizations have 24/7 hotlines where you can talk to trained pros who can offer immediate emotional support and coping strategies. They can also point you to more resources if you need them.
- **Self-Help Books and Resources**: There's a ton of books, websites, and online materials out there that can guide you through specific challenges. They're a great way to get new perspectives and tools to help you handle what's going on.
- **Faith-Based Communities**: If you're part of a religious or spiritual group, turning to your faith community can be a big source of comfort and support. They often provide counseling and resources that align with your beliefs.
- **Education and Training Programs**: Depending on what you're dealing with, educational programs or workshops can give you the know-how and skills to better understand and tackle your specific challenge. These could be about anything from managing money to reducing stress.
- **Peer Support Programs**: These programs connect you with people who've faced similar issues and come out the other side. They offer empathy, inspiration, and practical advice from someone who's been there.

Remember, it's okay to seek help when you're up against a challenge. The list above is a starting point, and different folks will find different resources more helpful, depending on what they need. Reaching out is a sign of strength, not weakness, and it can be the first step in navigating through your challenges successfully.

MAINTAINING A POSITIVE MINDSET:

IN LIFE, we often bump into challenges out of the blue – things like losing a job unexpectedly, facing a health scare, or dealing with personal issues. These situations can shake us up, but here's where keeping a positive mindset plays a huge role. Staying optimistic, being grateful, and having faith in ourselves are important for getting through these tough times and coming out stronger.

- **Optimism**: This is like the foundation of a positive mindset. It's all about believing that, somehow, things will turn out okay, even when it feels like everything's falling apart. Optimism helps us look for the good in bad situations and hang on to hope when things are messy. By staying optimistic, we see challenges as chances to grow and learn.
- **Gratitude**: Gratitude is a game-changer. It shifts our focus from what's going wrong to what's actually going right. When everything seems to be going sideways, it's easy to get stuck in a loop of negative thoughts. But practicing gratitude helps us spot the silver linings. Being thankful for even the small stuff can boost our mood and keep us hopeful.

- **Self-Belief**: This is about trusting ourselves and our abilities to get through tough times. When we're up against something unexpected, having self-belief means we stay focused on our goals and push forward with determination. It's about knowing deep down that we've got the strength and smarts to find solutions and move past obstacles.

Now, staying positive sounds great in theory, but how do you actually do it? Here are a couple of practical tips:

- **Positive Affirmations**: These are like little pep talks we give ourselves. Repeating encouraging statements like "I am strong, capable, and resilient" can change the way we think. It helps shift our mindset from negative to positive and keeps us focused on finding ways through our problems.
- **Visualization Exercises**: This is about picturing ourselves overcoming challenges and meeting our goals. When we imagine ourselves succeeding, it sends a powerful message to our subconscious that, yes, we can do this. It's a way of prepping our minds to handle and conquer tough situations.

Keeping a positive mindset when facing unexpected challenges isn't about ignoring the hard stuff. It's about recognizing the challenges but tackling them with optimism, gratitude, and a strong belief in ourselves. Regularly practicing things like affirmations and visualization can help us develop a resilient, positive mindset. And remember, it's often during tough times we discover our true strength and potential – and staying positive is key to unlocking that power.

SECTION ONE WRAP-UP:

INTRODUCTION TO UNEXPECTED CHALLENGES:

- Life is unpredictable with unexpected challenges.
- Importance of resilience and adaptability.
- The value of a support network.

Types of Unexpected Challenges:

- Personal setbacks (health, relationships, financial).
- Professional obstacles (workplace conflicts, tight deadlines).
- Sudden changes (natural disasters, global crises).

Emotional Impact of Unexpected Challenges:

- Emotional responses: fear, frustration, uncertainty.
- Strategies for managing emotions.

Overcoming Unexpected Challenges:

- Building resilience, problem-solving skills, and adaptability.
- Learning from challenges.

Learning and Growth:

- Adaptability, self-reflection, resilience, and growth mindset.
- Transformative experiences leading to personal development.

Support and Resources:

- Variety of support options: support groups, counseling, online communities.
- Importance of seeking help.

Maintaining a Positive Mindset:

- Optimism, gratitude, and self-belief as key elements.
- Techniques like positive affirmations and visualization exercises.

ACTION ITEMS:

Identify and Assess Challenges:

- Regularly reflect on personal and professional challenges.
- Classify challenges to understand their nature and impact.

Develop Emotional Management Strategies:

- Practice mindfulness and stress-reduction techniques.
- Seek emotional support when needed.

Enhance Resilience:

- Engage in activities that build mental and emotional strength.
- Regularly challenge yourself to step out of your comfort zone.

Cultivate Problem-Solving Skills:

- Go to workshops or take courses on creative problem-solving.
- Regularly brainstorm solutions for hypothetical situations.

Build a Support Network:

- Actively engage in community events or online forums.
- Establish connections with mentors or counselors.

Practice Self-Care and Self-Reflection:

- Maintain a routine for physical and mental health.
- Keep a journal for self-reflection and tracking growth.

Stay Optimistic and Grateful:

- Daily practice of noting things you are grateful for.
- Use positive affirmations to reinforce a positive mindset.

Use Available Resources:

- Research and bookmark resources relevant to potential challenges.
- Join groups or forums for shared experiences and support.

Regularly Evaluate and Adjust Approach:

- Review your strategies for handling challenges.
- Be open to adapting new methods or perspectives.

In Our Next Section:

In our next section, we'll be delving into the art of transforming challenges into springboards for success. Get ready to start an inspiring journey that showcases the incredible power of resilience, adaptability, and positive thinking. We'll be exploring real-life examples and practical strategies that show how facing and overcoming adversity can lead to remarkable personal growth and fulfillment. This section is designed not only to motivate you but also to give you the tools and insights you need to turn your own challenges into opportunities for triumph.

We'll be dissecting the anatomy of resilience, understanding its core parts, and learning how to cultivate it in our daily lives. Expect to dive deep into the realms of positive mindset, effective problem-solving, and the strength that comes from supportive relationships. This journey is about recognizing that each challenge we face is an opportunity to grow stronger, wiser, and more capable. So, gear up to be inspired, empowered, and equipped with the knowledge to not just survive life's storms, but to thrive in them. Your path to resilience and triumph awaits in the next exciting section!

SECTION TWO: RECOGNIZING AND ACCEPTING THE CHALLENGE

THIS SECTION EXPLORES why individuals must recognize the challenges they face to effectively address them.

UNDERSTANDING THE IMPORTANCE OF RECOGNIZING CHALLENGES:

UNDERSTANDING why it's important to spot the challenges in our lives is a big deal. It's like having a map – knowing what you're up against helps you navigate better and find the right path. Let's dive into why recognizing our challenges is key to personal growth and finding solutions that work.

- **Self-awareness**: When we look closely at the challenges we're facing, it's a chance to reflect and get to know ourselves. It's about figuring out our strengths, what we're not so great at, and where we might need to work. This self-knowledge is gold. It helps us get a clear picture of who we are and what areas of our life could use some sprucing up.
- **Problem-solving**: Identifying challenges is step one in solving them. Once we know what the hurdles are, we can think about ways to jump over them. This approach means we're dealing with the real root, not just slapping a quick fix on the symptoms.
- **Personal Growth**: Every challenge is a chance to stretch ourselves and grow. When we face these challenges head-on, we step out of our comfort zones, pick up new skills, and

collect experiences that make us better at handling whatever comes next. These growth moments are important – they don't just help us with the current problem but also gear us up for future ones.

- **Empowerment**: Realizing what we're up against gives us power. Instead of feeling tossed around by life, we get to take charge and actively work on getting past these obstacles. This shift in mindset builds resilience and confidence, making us more determined and proactive when tackling challenges.
- **Building Relationships**: Being aware of our own challenges helps us build stronger, more supportive connections with others. When we know what we're struggling with, we can communicate better, ask for help, and offer support to others in similar boats. Opening up about our challenges can create a sense of community and teamwork, making it easier to find solutions together.
- **Focusing on Needs**: Knowing our challenges helps us figure out what needs our immediate attention. It's all about focusing our energy and resources on the things that matter and will make the biggest difference in our lives.

Recognizing the challenges we face is important for personal growth, solving problems effectively, and overall well-being. It puts us in the driver's seat of our lives, helps us find solutions that work, and strengthens our relationships. By embracing our challenges, we turn them into opportunities for growth and lead more fulfilling lives.

IDENTIFYING PERSONAL CHALLENGES:

DIGGING deep into ourselves and being aware of our thoughts and feelings is like having a superpower. It helps us get to know ourselves and figure out the challenges we're facing. This chapter is all about the importance of introspection and self-awareness and how they can guide us in identifying and tackling our personal obstacles.

Sometimes, we might feel like we're stuck or overwhelmed and can't put our finger on why. This is where not being in tune with ourselves can hold us back from finding solutions and growing. But, if we take the time for some introspection, we can start to unravel our emotions, thoughts, and behaviors.

- **Introspection**: This is all about looking inward and being honest with ourselves about our motivations, beliefs, and values. When we reflect on ourselves, we can spot patterns and triggers, and uncover the deeper issues that might be at the heart of our challenges. It's about taking charge of our experiences and making choices that reflect who we are.
- **Self-Awareness**: This goes further than just understanding what's going on inside us. It's about knowing how our thoughts and actions affect not only ourselves but also the

people around us. Self-awareness lets us see our strengths and the areas we need to work on. It helps us navigate our relationships, make decisions that fit our values, and handle challenges in a way that works for us.

By embracing both introspection and self-awareness, we get better at spotting the unique challenges we face. These challenges are often shaped by our own experiences, personalities, and life situations. The only way to get a handle on these challenges is by taking the time to explore and understand ourselves.

Recognizing our specific challenges is a big first step toward solving them. It lets us tailor our approach, find the right resources and support, and tackle these issues in a way that suits us best. Without this self-awareness, we might try one-size-fits-all solutions that don't get us anywhere.

Plus, introspection and self-awareness give us a sense of control and the reminder that we have the power to change and grow. They show us that our challenges don't define us. With this understanding, we can adopt a proactive attitude, take the reins of our life, and actively work toward making things better.

The role of introspection and self-awareness in recognizing and addressing our personal challenges is important. By taking a deep dive into our own minds and hearts, we can uncover and confront the root causes of our struggles. This process helps us make choices right for us, find strategies that fit our unique needs, and seek the support we need to overcome these challenges. Introspection and self-awareness equip us with everything we need to live fulfilling and meaningful lives.

ACCEPTING THE REALITY OF CHALLENGES:

IN LIFE, we often run into challenges that feel like giant mountains blocking our path. These can be anything from personal issues to work problems, and sometimes they can seem overwhelming. Our first instinct might be to push back against these challenges or try to dodge them, but real growth and resilience actually come from accepting and embracing them.

- **Acceptance**: This is all about acknowledging and coming to terms with what's happening. It's not throwing in the towel; it's more like recognizing what's in front of us and being okay with it. It means understanding that some things are out of our hands and resisting them only leads to more stress and disappointment.
- **Seeing Challenges as Opportunities**: Once we accept our situation, we start to see challenges in a new light. Instead of roadblocks, they become chances for us to grow and transform. Acceptance shifts our mindset, turning an obstacle into a learning opportunity and a way to become a better version of ourselves.

- **Embracing Challenges**: This means looking for ways to get past the hurdle. Instead of getting bogged down by the negative or feeling swamped, we focus our energy on finding solutions and making moves. Taking on a challenge needs guts, grit, and the readiness to step outside what's comfortable.
- **Acceptance and Action**: Acceptance is the first step; it lays the groundwork for our action plan. It clears our head so we can look at the situation and figure out what to do next. But remember, accepting isn't about sitting back. It's about seeing things for what they are and then getting proactive to work through them.
- **Beyond Overcoming Challenges**: Embracing and accepting challenges isn't just about getting past them. It's about recognizing that they're a natural part of life. By tackling these challenges head-on, we find new strengths, pick up new skills, and tap into abilities we didn't even know we had.

When we accept and embrace the challenges that come our way, we start developing a mindset that sees setbacks as bridges. We learn to adjust, get creative, and keep going even when things are tough. We turn into more resilient people, not just getting through challenges but thriving because of them.

Accepting and embracing challenges is key to our growth and success. It's through accepting that we gain the insight we need to get through tough times. And by embracing these challenges, we turn them into chances for growth, setting us up to overcome obstacles and reach our full potential. So, let's welcome the challenges we face – they're what help us grow into stronger, smarter people.

DEVELOPING A POSITIVE MINDSET:

RUNNING into challenges and obstacles is a standard part of life. They test our patience, resilience, and determination. But it's not the challenges themselves that decide how things turn out – it's all about how we think about and perceive these challenges. This chapter is all about the power of having a positive mindset and how it can turn hurdles into building blocks for growth and success. By learning to see challenges in a new light, we can handle them with ease and grow as individuals.

- **The Influence of Mindset**: Our mindset is important in how we deal with challenges. With a positive mindset, we can see these challenges as chances to grow. If we're stuck in a negative mindset, though, it can slow us down and stop us from reaching our full potential. Understanding the power of our mindset is key because our thoughts and beliefs do shape our reality.
- **Reframing Challenges as Opportunities**: One great way to stay positive is to think of challenges not as roadblocks but as opportunities. This change in perspective can be a game-

changer. It lets us approach challenges with excitement and curiosity, ready to find the growth and learning they offer.

- **Embracing a Growth Mindset**: Having a growth mindset means believing we can develop our abilities and intelligence with effort and practice. When we adopt this mindset, we see challenges as a normal and important part of learning. They become chances to improve, learn more, and stretch our abilities.
- **Developing Resilience**: Resilience is all about bouncing back from tough times and keeping on going in the face of challenges. A positive mindset is a big help here because it lets us see setbacks as temporary, not permanent. We learn from our mistakes, adapt, and come back even stronger.
- **Practicing Positive Self-Talk**: The way we talk to ourselves matters. Positive self-talk can help us push past self-doubt and negative thoughts, especially when we're facing challenges. Repeating positive affirmations and encouraging ourselves can boost our confidence and remind us of our strengths.
- **Surrounding Yourself with Positive Influences**: The people around us and our environment have a huge impact on our mindset. By hanging out with positive people, seeking mentors, or diving into motivational materials, we can keep our mindset upbeat. These positive influences give us support and encouragement when we're up against something tough.

To wrap it up, having a positive mindset is important for handling life's challenges. By seeing challenges as chances for growth, keeping a growth mindset, building resilience, practicing positive self-talk, and surrounding ourselves with good vibes, we can face obstacles with optimism and resilience. These approaches transform challenges into valuable experiences that help us grow and succeed. Adopting these strategies can change the game on our journey toward personal growth and success.

BUILDING RESILIENCE:

RESILIENCE IS like a superpower that helps us handle tough times with grace and determination. It's all about bouncing back from rough patches and turning those experiences into personal growth and success. Let's dive into what resilience is all about, why it's so important in dealing with challenges, and share tips on how to build and strengthen this awesome trait in our lives.

- **Understanding Resilience**: First off, resilience isn't something you're born with – it's a skill you can develop. It's about keeping a positive attitude, being emotionally flexible, and always looking for ways to grow. Resilient folks see challenges as chances to learn, not as huge roadblocks. This mindset gives them the confidence to handle setbacks and keep moving forward.
- **The Role of Resilience in Accepting Challenges**: Embracing challenges is key to both personal and professional growth. Resilience is what lets us face these challenges head-on instead of running away from them. It helps us recognize our limits and understand that stumbling sometimes is part of life. Tackling challenges with resilience boosts our self-confidence

and problem-solving skills and makes us more open to taking risks.

- **Overcoming Challenges with Resilience**: When we hit a bump in the road, resilience helps us get back up and keep going. Here are strategies to help build resilience:
- **Cultivating a Positive Mindset**: Keep an eye out for the silver linings in tough situations. Focus on what you can control and look for chances to learn and grow.
- **Building a Support Network**: Surround yourself with people who lift you up and can offer good advice when you're facing challenges. Their support and perspective can be a huge help.
- **Practicing Self-Care**: Don't forget to take care of yourself – physically, emotionally, and mentally. Do things that make you happy, help you relax, and keep you healthy. Regular exercise, eating well, and getting enough sleep are key.
- **Setting Realistic Goals**: Break big goals into smaller steps and celebrate your victories along the way. This helps build confidence and keeps you motivated.
- **Learning from Setbacks**: Instead of getting hung up on what went wrong, focus on what you can learn from each setback. Think about how you can do better next time and use your experiences to improve.
- **Embracing Change and Adversity**: Change is a part of life, so try to see it as a chance to grow. Adapting to change is important for resilience, and facing adversity is an opportunity to learn new skills and broaden your horizons.

Resilience is important when dealing with life's challenges. By developing resilience, we can face setbacks with a can-do attitude, embrace change, and always look for growth opportunities. By staying positive, building a support network, taking care of ourselves, setting achievable goals, learning from our mistakes, and being open to change, we can strengthen our resilience and tackle life's ups and downs with confidence. Resilience is what powers us to bounce back from tough times and keep moving toward our personal and professional goals.

SEEKING SUPPORT:

WHEN WE BUMP into challenges and tough spots in life, it's common to feel swamped and unsure. That's exactly when realizing the importance of seeking support from others makes a huge difference. Getting advice, guidance, or having someone there for you can give you the extra boost you need to get through those rough patches.

- **Seeking Support is Courageous**: Asking for help isn't a weakness; it's actually a brave and smart move. Understanding that we're not meant to tackle everything solo is a big step toward personal growth and resilience. When we open up to others for support, we're building a network of people who genuinely care about our well-being.
- **Gaining Insight and Wisdom**: One of the best parts about seeking support is the different perspectives and experiences others can offer. Talking to a mentor, friend, or family member can shine a new light on our situation. They might have advice from their own life or suggest solutions we hadn't thought of. This input can be really eye-opening and help us make better decisions.

- **A Space to Vent**: Keeping all our feelings bottled up isn't great for our mental and emotional health. Talking things out with someone creates a safe space where we can let it all out without being judged. Saying what's on our mind can clear things up and take a load off our shoulders. A compassionate ear can be comforting and give us the release we need.
- **Encouragement and Motivation**: The support and encouragement from those around us can be a real game-changer. When we're on our own, self-doubt can creep in pretty easily. But having people in our corner reminds us of what we're capable of, boosting our confidence and giving us the push we need.
- **Building Connections and Community**: Reaching out for support strengthens our relationships and makes us feel more connected. We're social creatures and feeling like we're part of a community is important. When we ask for help, we're also encouraging others to do the same. This give-and-take creates a solid network of support that goes beyond our own challenges.

To wrap it up, asking for help is a key part of growing and staying resilient. Acknowledging that we can't go it alone opens up the world of support, wisdom, and encouragement from others. Seeking support not only brings us valuable insights but also reminds us that we're not alone in this. So let's embrace the strength it takes to ask for help and cherish the relationships that keep us going, especially during tough times.

~

EMBRACING CHANGE: A PATH TO OVERCOMING CHALLENGES

LIFE's full of ups and downs, from little hiccups to big roadblocks. How we deal with these challenges often shapes our success and personal growth. A key ingredient in getting over these hurdles is embracing change. When we see change as a normal part of life and stay open to new things, we're arming ourselves with everything we need to tackle any challenge.

Change is always happening, whether it's in our environment, relationships, or personal lives. Sure, it can be scary and uncomfortable, but it's also packed with chances for new beginnings and growth. Stepping out of our comfort zones and keeping an open mind lets us explore different ideas and paths. Like Alan Watts, the British philosopher, said, "The only way to make sense out of change is to plunge into it, move with it, and join the dance." Resisting change means we miss out on opportunities to adapt and grow. Embracing it means we're riding the wave of life, not fighting against it.

When we're up against a challenge, it's important to remember that change isn't the enemy; it's actually our ally. Challenges often come up when we're stuck in old ways that don't work anymore. Being open to change brings in fresh ideas and new ways of thinking that can help us solve problems in innovative ways.

Plus, embracing change is a huge part of personal growth. Venturing into unknown territory helps us build resilience, flexibility, and adaptability. These aren't just useful for the challenge at hand; they're skills we can use in all parts of life.

Embracing change also means breaking free from limiting beliefs and habits that hold us back. It encourages us to reevaluate our views and try different strategies, promoting a mindset of continuous learning and growth.

Although it might feel daunting at first, diving into change is where we often find our true strengths. It opens us up to new talents, passions, and abilities we might not have known we had. Change is a powerful force that drives personal and professional growth, pushing us forward in our journey of discovery and fulfillment.

So, briefly, embracing change is important for overcoming challenges. By staying open to new situations, adapting our approach, and exploring different possibilities, we're setting ourselves up for success. Life is all about evolving, and by welcoming change, we can navigate through challenges, uncover new opportunities, and start a fulfilling path of growth.

~

SECTION TWO WRAP-UP:

UNDERSTANDING the Importance of Recognizing Challenges:

- Recognizing challenges is essential for self-awareness and problem-solving.
- It enables personal growth and empowerment.
- Acknowledges the role of challenges in building relationships and focusing on needs.

Identifying Personal Challenges:

- Emphasizes introspection and self-awareness for recognizing personal obstacles.
- Highlights the importance of understanding one's thoughts, feelings, and behaviors.

Accepting the Reality of Challenges:

- Importance of acceptance in facing challenges.

- Seeing challenges as opportunities for growth.
- Embracing challenges leads to proactive actions and beyond.

Developing a Positive Mindset:

- The role of mindset in overcoming challenges.
- Reframing challenges as opportunities.
- Embracing a growth mindset and developing resilience.

Building Resilience:

- Understanding and developing resilience.
- Importance of a positive mindset, support network, self-care, goal setting, and learning from setbacks.

Seeking Support:

- Recognizing the value of seeking support.
- Benefits of external perspectives, emotional expression, and motivation.
- Building connections and community through seeking support.

Embracing Change:

- Viewing change as an ally in overcoming challenges.
- Role of change in personal growth and breaking free from limiting beliefs.

ACTION ITEMS:

Set Clear Goals for Recognizing Challenges:

- Regularly assess personal and professional challenges.
- Identify patterns in behavior and triggers.

Engage in Self-Reflection Exercises:

- Give time for introspection.
- Practice mindfulness and journaling.

Practice Acceptance of Challenges:

- Acknowledge and articulate the challenges faced.
- Cultivate a mindset that views challenges as growth opportunities.

Cultivate a Positive Mindset:

- Implement daily positive affirmations.
- Visualize successful outcomes.

Work on Building Resilience:

- Participate in activities that build mental and emotional strength.
- Establish a routine of self-care and goal setting.

Actively Seek and Offer Support:

- Join support groups or communities.
- Engage in meaningful conversations with mentors or peers.

Embrace and Initiate Change:

- Challenge yourself to step out of your comfort zone.
- Adapt to new situations and learn from them.
- **Continuously Evaluate and Adapt Strategies:**
- Regularly review and adjust approaches to challenges.
- Stay open to learning from experiences and feedback.

In Our Next Section:

In Our Next Section: Transforming Challenges into Steppingstones

As we venture into our next section, we'll dig deeper into the transformative power of embracing life's challenges. We've navigated through recognizing and understanding the hurdles we face, both personally and professionally. Now, it's time to turn these obstacles into steppingstones for our growth and success. We'll explore innovative strategies that go beyond coping and resilience, focusing on how to transform our struggles into fuel for our aspirations. This journey is about more than just overcoming; it's about redefining our approach to life's challenges, turning them into opportunities that propel us forward.

Get ready to be inspired and equipped with practical tools that will not only help you tackle life's unexpected twists and turns but also empower you to thrive in the face of adversity. We'll share inspiring stories of triumph and offer actionable advice you can apply in your daily life. This next section is designed to motivate you to see challenges in a new light, as catalysts for personal and professional growth. Embrace this journey with an open heart and mind and prepare to transform the way you perceive and conquer the challenges ahead. Let's step into this new chapter together, ready to turn every challenge into a chance for unparalleled growth and achievement.

SECTION THREE: NAVIGATING LIFE'S CHALLENGES:

EMBRACING LIFE'S LEVEL-UPS

LET'S FACE IT – life isn't always a walk in the park. We all bump into personal and professional hurdles that test our strength and problem-solving abilities. In this chapter, we'll look at different challenges people often face and talk about why it's important to recognize and understand them to effectively deal with life's tough moments.

Types of Challenges: Challenges come in all shapes and sizes, and they hit everyone differently. Here are a few common ones:

- **Personal challenges**: These are things like health problems, issues in relationships, money troubles, or dealing with loss. They can shake up our daily life and well-being.
- **Professional challenges**: At work, challenges might be job uncertainty, heavy workloads, or tricky dynamics with coworkers or bosses. These challenges can affect how happy we are at work and even impact our career progress.
- **Educational challenges**: For students, it's often about academic pressure, tough subjects, or finding motivation. These challenges can play a big role in their performance, confidence, and future opportunities.

Recognizing and Understanding Challenges The first step in handling these challenges is to recognize and understand them. That means admitting when we're facing a tough time, figuring out what's causing it, and getting a handle on what each challenge involves. Understanding our challenges helps us figure out the best way to tackle them.

Importance of Recognizing Challenges There are a lot of good things that come from acknowledging our challenges. Here's why it's so important:

- **Taking Action**: Recognizing a challenge means we can stop avoiding the issue and start dealing with it. This might mean getting professional help, finding ways to cope, or changing our situation.
- **Personal Growth**: Challenges are often chances to grow. By facing them head-on, we can learn a lot, build our resilience, and get to know our strengths.
- **Building Support Networks**: When we're open about our challenges, we're more likely to reach out for help. Having a strong support network is key to getting through tough times.

Navigating Through Challenges Once we've got a good grip on our challenges, we can start using strategies to get past them. Here are solid approaches:

- **Setting Realistic Goals**: Tackling challenges bit by bit makes them less daunting. Focus on small, achievable goals to keep your motivation up and gain momentum.
- **Seeking Support**: Don't be afraid to lean on family, friends, mentors, or counselors for advice and encouragement.
- **Practicing Self-Care**: Taking care of yourself is important. Things like exercising, meditating, enjoying hobbies, or spending time with loved ones can keep you balanced.
- **Embracing a Growth Mindset**: Try to see challenges as opportunities to learn and improve, not just as barriers.

Changing the way we think about challenges can make us more resilient and creative.

Conclusion Challenges are a normal part of life, both personally and professionally. By recognizing and understanding them, we can tackle them proactively, seek support, and use effective strategies to get through. Doing this not only helps us overcome these challenges but also helps us grow, become more resilient, and prepare for whatever else life has in store.

IMPACT OF PERSONAL CHALLENGES:

PERSONAL CHALLENGES CAN SHAKE things up in our lives, touching everything from our overall well-being to how we perform at work. These challenges come in different shapes and sizes, like health problems, issues in our relationships, or money troubles, and they can throw a wrench into our work life.

- **Health Issues**: If you're dealing with a health problem, it can make focusing and being effective at work tough. Chronic illnesses or constant pain can leave you feeling exhausted and less sharp, which can hit your productivity. Plus, having to take time off for doctor appointments or treatments can disrupt your work routine and pile on more stress.
- **Relationship Problems**: When things aren't great with a spouse, family member, or close friend, it can spill over into your job. The emotional stress from ongoing relationship issues can make it hard to concentrate at work or get along with coworkers. And all that stress and worry can zap your motivation and make you feel less engaged with your job.
- **Financial Difficulties**: Money problems are another big personal challenge that can affect your work. Constantly

worrying about money can make it hard to focus on your job. And if you're trying to juggle extra work or longer hours to make ends meet, you could feel burned out.

These personal challenges don't just affect how you do at work; they can hit your mental and emotional health too. The stress and pressure from these issues can lead to anxiety, depression, and other mental health struggles, which all affect how well you can perform professionally. These challenges can also drain your energy and motivation, leaving you feeling less satisfied with your job.

Given how much personal challenges can affect professional life, it's important for workplaces to offer support. Employers can help out by providing flexible work arrangements, counseling services, or employee assistance programs. This support can make a big difference in helping people deal with personal issues while keeping a healthy balance between work and life. Creating a supportive work environment where people feel comfortable talking about their challenges without fear of judgment is also key.

To sum it up, personal challenges like health issues, relationship problems, or financial troubles can seriously affect our well-being and how we do at work. Recognizing and dealing with these challenges is important for staying productive and happy in our jobs. Workplaces that offer support and resources can help their employees navigate through these personal challenges and maintain a positive and productive work atmosphere.

IMPACT OF PROFESSIONAL CHALLENGES:

IN TODAY'S fast-paced work world, it's common to see how job-related challenges can spill over into our personal lives and affect our overall happiness. The demands of many jobs, along with long hours and high expectations, can be a lot to handle, both mentally and emotionally.

- **Heavy Workload**: One big issue for a lot of folks is just how much work they must do. With deadlines, assignments, and responsibilities constantly piling up, the pressure to get everything done can be overwhelming. This often means sacrificing time with family and friends, missing out on important events, or just not switching off from work mode. This can strain relationships and chip away at your overall happiness.
- **Toxic Work Environments**: Dealing with difficult coworkers or bosses can take a toll. It can lead to stress, anxiety, and sometimes even depression. When your work environment is negative, it's hard to keep that from affecting your personal life too. It can eat away at your self-esteem and make it tough to find joy in other parts of your life.

- **Job Security Concerns**: Worrying about job security is another big stressor. The fear of losing your job can hang over you, overshadowing the good things in life. This uncertainty can put a strain on personal relationships and make it hard to enjoy the present.
- **Burnout**: When you're constantly facing challenges like too much work, a negative workplace, or job insecurity, burnout can sneak up on you. Burnout means feeling exhausted, cynical, and like you're just not achieving much. It doesn't just stay at work, either – it can affect every part of your life, making it hard to find satisfaction or happiness anywhere.

The impact of work challenges on our personal lives and happiness is real. Stress, burnout, and feelings of not being good enough can creep into every part of our lives. This can lead to strained relationships, low self-esteem, and a general lack of fulfillment. That's why it's so important to look after ourselves and get help when we need it, whether that's through self-care or professional support. Addressing these work challenges is key to taking back control of our personal lives and finding true happiness.

STRATEGIES FOR MANAGING CHALLENGES:

MANAGING CHALLENGES, be it in your personal or professional life, can sometimes feel like a juggling act. But hey, with the right strategies and know-how, you can get through these tough times. Here are handy tips to help you manage challenges more effectively:

- **Practice Self-Care**: First things first, look after yourself. When you're up against a challenge, do things that make you happy and help you unwind. This could work out, diving into your hobbies, meditating, or hanging out with your favorite people. Giving yourself time to recharge is key to staying strong and ready to tackle whatever comes your way.
- **Seek Support**: Remember, you're not in this alone. Contact friends, family, or coworkers when you need a chat or some advice. Sometimes, just talking about a problem can give you a whole new perspective. And if things get tough, think about getting some professional help, like seeing a therapist or counselor. Having someone to talk to can make a world of difference.
- **Set Boundaries**: It's okay to say no sometimes. Setting boundaries is all about knowing your limits and putting your

needs first when you need to. Let people know what you can and can't take on, and don't shy away from delegating tasks or asking for help when you need it. Setting clear boundaries is a great way to avoid burnout and keep your energy levels up for dealing with challenges.

- **Develop Resilience**: Being resilient means bouncing back from tough times. Try to see challenges as chances to learn and grow. Keep a positive attitude, focus on finding solutions, and be open to changing your approach if needed. Building resilience doesn't happen overnight, but it's definitely worth the effort and will help you handle challenges much more smoothly.
- **Focus on and Organize**: When things get hectic, it's important to figure out what needs your attention first. List what you need to do and break bigger tasks into smaller steps. Getting organized like this helps you make a clear plan of action and stops you from feeling swamped.
- **Learn from Setbacks**: Setbacks are just part of life, and they're actually great opportunities to learn. If you hit a roadblock, take some time to think about what went wrong and what you can learn from it. Use these experiences to improve and keep moving forward. Adopting a growth mindset and seeing challenges as learning experiences will help you overcome obstacles with more resilience and determination.

Handling challenges, whether in your personal or work life, comes down to a proactive and balanced approach. By taking good care of yourself, reaching out for help, setting clear boundaries, building up your resilience, staying organized, and learning from your setbacks, you can tackle challenges head-on and come out stronger. Remember, challenges are a normal part of life, but with the right strategies and attitude, you can get through them.

BUILDING RESILIENCE:

THIS CHAPTER IS all about why it's important to build resilience. You know, that ability to bounce back from tough times and actually come out of them stronger and wiser. Resilience isn't just about making it through the rough patches; it's about growing from those experiences.

- **Developing a Positive Mindset**: One big part of building resilience is keeping a positive outlook, even when things get tricky. Studies have shown that a positive attitude can really amp up our ability to tackle challenges. Training ourselves to see the brighter side of things helps us stay optimistic and boosts our confidence in our problem-solving skills.
- **Practicing Self-Reflection**: Taking time to think about our thoughts, feelings, and actions is key to understanding our strengths and weaknesses. It also helps us spot any patterns or triggers that might hold us back. This self-reflection deepens our self-awareness and equips us with strategies to manage stress and handle difficult situations more effectively.
- **Cultivating a Growth-Oriented Attitude**: Seeing challenges as chances to learn and grow is another important part of resilience. If we approach tough situations with the mindset

that they're just temporary hurdles, we can keep pushing forward and adapt our plans to overcome them.

- **Focusing on Self-Care**: Let's not forget about taking care of ourselves. Looking after our physical and mental health gives us the strength and energy we need to face challenges head-on. Doing things like exercising, meditating, spending time with loved ones, or enjoying hobbies is all about recharging and keeping our emotional tank full.
- **Building a Support Network**: Having people you can rely on for advice and encouragement makes a big difference. Friends, family, mentors – they're all part of a support system that can boost our ability to get through tough times. These connections provide a sense of belonging and an extra layer of resilience.

To wrap it up, building resilience is all about getting better at coping with and bouncing back from life's challenges. By focusing on the positives, reflecting on ourselves, embracing growth, taking good care of ourselves, and leaning on our support network, we can face adversity with more resilience and grace. It's all about equipping ourselves with the right tools to handle whatever life throws our way.

CASE STUDIES:

THIS CHAPTER DIVES into some incredible stories of people who've faced big personal and professional challenges and came out on top. These stories aren't just inspiring; they show us how adversity can be a springboard for growth and personal development.

Note: These stories are fictional, based on real life stories for illustrative purposes.

Case Study 1: Anna's Journey to Self-Acceptance Meet Anna, a young woman in her early 20s. She's always struggled with low self-esteem, especially about her looks. Growing up, she felt judged and didn't quite match up to society's beauty standards, which hit her confidence.

But Anna didn't let this keep her down. She turned her challenges into a chance to grow. She started journaling about her insecurities, digging into why she felt this way, and even got professional therapy. Slowly but surely, Anna began to accept and love herself just as she is, embracing her uniqueness and building her confidence from within.

Anna's journey didn't stop there. She started a blog to share her story and inspire others facing similar issues. The positive feedback she got motivated her even more, and she eventually became a life coach, helping people overcome their own self-esteem struggles and find self-acceptance.

Case Study 2: John's Career Transition Triumph Then there's John, who always wanted a creative career but ended up in finance. He felt stuck and unfulfilled, his passion tucked away.

Deciding enough was enough, John took a bold step toward his dream. It wasn't easy – he faced the fear of the unknown, had to pick up new skills, and even took a pay cut to start anew in a creative agency. But John was determined, and his hard work and persistence paid off. He learned, networked, and threw himself into his new field, eventually becoming a successful creative director.

John's story is a powerful example of following your passion and daring to change your path. He's an inspiration for anyone looking to break free from what's expected and chase what makes them happy.

Through these case studies, we get a real sense of how to tackle personal and professional challenges. These stories show us the importance of resilience, self-reflection, and stepping out of our comfort zones. With determination and the right mindset, we can turn tough situations into chances for success and personal growth.

In wrapping up this section, we've seen how challenges can shape us. They push us, test our resilience, and help us develop in ways we might not have imagined. The key takeaway? Embrace challenges. By facing them head-on, we open ourselves to new strengths and a sense of achievement.

We also talked about how to deal with challenges – reaching out for support, taking care of ourselves, and keeping a positive outlook. Using these strategies can help us manage life's tough spots more effectively.

Remember, challenges might be tough, but they're also opportunities to grow and succeed. So, as you move forward, don't shy away from them. Step out of your comfort zone, face difficulties, and keep the coping mechanisms from this chapter in mind. You'll not only grow personally and professionally but also build a foundation for lasting success. Challenges are tough but they're not impossible to overcome. Embrace them, conquer them, and let them make you stronger and more resilient.

SECTION THREE WRAP-UP:

Introduction to Challenges

- **Life's Hurdles**: Personal and professional challenges test our resilience and problem-solving abilities.
- **Types of Challenges**: Include personal issues, work-related problems, and academic pressures.

Recognizing and Understanding Challenges

- **First Step**: Acknowledging and understanding challenges is important for effective management.
- **Benefits of Recognition**: Leads to action, personal growth, stronger support networks, and better prioritization.

Navigating Through Challenges

- **Tackling Challenges**: Involves setting goals, seeking support, practicing self-care, and adopting a growth mindset.

Impact of Personal Challenges

- **Influence on Work and Well-being**: Health issues, relationship problems, and financial difficulties can affect job performance and mental health.

Impact of Professional Challenges

- **Work-Life Balance**: Heavy workloads, toxic environments, and job insecurity can affect personal happiness and mental health.

Strategies for Managing Challenges

- **Effective Management**: Includes self-care, support seeking, setting boundaries, developing resilience, focusing on, and learning from setbacks.

Building Resilience

- **Growth and Coping**: Developing a positive mindset, self-reflection, embracing growth attitudes, self-care, and creating support networks enhances resilience.

ACTION ITEMS:

Recognizing Challenges

- **Reflect Regularly**: Take time to identify and understand ongoing personal and professional challenges.
- **Journaling**: Write down thoughts and feelings to better understand personal struggles.

Navigating Challenges

- **Set Small Goals**: Break down challenges into manageable goals.
- **Seek Counseling**: If overwhelmed, consider professional counseling for guidance.

Personal Challenges

- **Health Management**: Regular check-ups and healthy lifestyle choices to manage health-related challenges.
- **Communication in Relationships**: Engage in open and honest dialogues with partners or family to address relationship issues.
- **Financial Planning**: Seek financial advice or create a budget plan for money-related challenges.

Professional Challenges

- **Work-Life Balance**: Allocate specific times for work and personal life to avoid burnout.
- **Conflict Resolution Skills**: Learn techniques to handle difficult work situations effectively.

Managing Challenges

- **Time Management**: Use tools like planners to organize tasks and reduce workload stress.
- **Professional Development**: Take courses or workshops to enhance problem-solving skills.

Building Resilience

- **Positive Affirmations**: Regularly practice positive self-talk to boost confidence and resilience.
- **Join Support Groups**: Engage with groups for shared experiences and coping strategies.

Upcoming Strategies

- **Face Challenges Head-On**: Embrace challenges as opportunities for growth.
- **Resilience Building**: Continue developing resilience through various personal and professional experiences.
- **Coping Mechanisms**: Implement coping mechanisms discussed in this chapter in daily life challenges.
- **Seek Opportunities in Adversity**: Look for learning and growth opportunities in every challenge faced.

In Our Next Section:

In our next section, we'll start a journey to harness the full potential of resilience in our lives. It's about transforming the way we perceive and tackle life's challenges. We'll dig into practical strategies that not only enhance our ability to bounce back from adversity but also empower us to thrive amidst it. This is your opportunity to turn resilience into your superpower, a tool that not only helps you withstand the storms but also guides you to navigate through them with wisdom and strength.

Get ready to explore the realms of self-improvement and personal growth. We'll focus on actionable steps to reinforce your resilience, from refining problem-solving skills to embracing change with open arms. This section is designed to inspire and equip you with the tools you need to face life's uncertainties with confidence and poise. Join us as we uncover the secrets to a resilient life, where challenges are viewed as stepping stones to greater heights, and every setback is an opportunity for a remarkable comeback. Let's turn your resilience into an unstoppable force that shapes a fulfilling and successful life.

SECTION FOUR: STRATEGIES FOR DEVELOPING RESILIENCE

UNDERSTANDING THE CONCEPT OF RESILIENCE:

RESILIENCE IS like this superpower we all have the potential to develop. It's about bouncing back from tough times and not just getting through them, but actually growing stronger and wiser because of them. We all face setbacks and challenges, but it's the resilient folks who manage to overcome these hurdles, learn from them, and keep on thriving.

- **Emotional Regulation**: A big part of resilience is handling our emotions well. Resilient people can work through negative feelings and cope with them in healthy ways, instead of getting bogged down. This emotional control helps them stay hopeful and optimistic, even when things look grim.
- **Problem Solving and Decision Making**: Resilience also involves being good at thinking through problems and making smart choices. When resilient people hit a rough patch, they can look at the situation, weigh their options, and come up with creative solutions. They don't get stuck in negativity or hopelessness; they adapt and find new ways to move forward.
- **Impact on Relationships and Social Interactions**: Resilience doesn't just help us personally; it's also important for our relationships and how we interact with others. Resilient people

usually have strong, healthy connections. They're good at handling conflicts, understanding different points of view, and communicating clearly. Being resilient means building a network of support and making positive contributions to the community.

- **Personal Growth and Development**: Here's where resilience shines. It's all about seeing failures and setbacks as chances to grow. Resilient people have this growth mindset – they embrace challenges, keep going after their goals, and don't see difficulties as signs they're not good enough. Facing challenges head-on builds self-confidence, sharpens skills, and leads to valuable experiences that help both personally and professionally.

To build up resilience, it's key to have a strong support network, surround yourself with positivity, and take care of yourself. Things like exercising, practicing mindfulness, and getting professional help when you need it can all play a part. Building resilience is a journey that takes effort and self-reflection, but the benefits are huge.

Wrapping it up, resilience is all about recovering from tough times and keeping a positive, hopeful outlook. It helps us manage our emotions, think through problems, build strong relationships, and grow as individuals. It's a cornerstone of personal growth and success, teaching us to learn from setbacks and come out stronger. By embracing resilience, we can tackle life's challenges with more strength and confidence, setting ourselves up for a fulfilling, rewarding life.

~

IDENTIFYING PERSONAL STRENGTHS AND WEAKNESSES:

IN THIS CHAPTER, we will take a deep dive into self-reflection and self-awareness, and how they help us pinpoint our strengths and weaknesses. Understanding ourselves is the bedrock of building resilience. It's all about knowing what we're good at and where we might need a little work.

Understanding Self-Reflection and Its Role: Let's talk about self-reflection first. It's like stepping back and looking at your thoughts, feelings, and actions from the outside. When we reflect on ourselves, we see patterns in our behavior and understand why we do what we do. This helps us make better choices moving forward.

To help with self-reflection, we've got exercises and techniques lined up for you. These activities are all about exploring your values, what you believe in, and how you react in different situations. By doing this, you can see what drives you and influences your decisions.

The 'Three Whys' Technique: When you encounter a strong emotion or reaction, ask yourself 'why' three times to delve deeper into your initial responses. For example, if you're feeling anxious about a meeting, asking 'why' repeatedly could reveal underlying concerns about preparedness or being judged.

Mood Mapping: At different points in the day, note down your mood and the activities or thoughts associated with it. Over time, this can reveal patterns in what influences your mood swings.

Reflection Prompts: Use specific prompts to guide your journaling. Examples include:

- What lesson did I learn today and how can I apply it?
- What am I grateful for today and why?
- Did I live according to my core values today? How so?

Life Satisfaction Wheel: Draw a circle and divide it into segments representing different life areas (work, relationships, health, etc.). Rate your satisfaction in each area and reflect on why some areas score higher or lower.

Conversation Replay: Think about a recent conversation that was significant. Write down what was said and then reflect on:

- What were your feelings during the conversation?
- What might you have misunderstood or assumed?
- How might you handle a similar conversation differently?

Goal Reflection: Regularly review your short and long-term goals. Ask yourself:

- Why are these goals important?
- How am I progressing toward these goals?
- What obstacles am I facing, and how can I overcome them?

Personal SWOT Analysis: Do a SWOT (Strengths, Weaknesses, Opportunities, Threats) analysis on yourself. Reflect on how your strengths can be leveraged more and how to address your weaknesses.

Visual Journaling: Sometimes words aren't enough. Use drawing, painting, or collage to express your feelings and thoughts. Reflect on what these visuals reveal about your inner state.

Mirror Exercise: Stand in front of a mirror and talk to yourself about your day. Observe your facial expressions and body language. What do they tell you about how you feel?

'Letter to Myself' Exercise: Write a letter to your future self, outlining your current state, aspirations, and fears. Alternatively, write a letter from your future self to your current self, offering advice and perspective.

'Day in Review' Exercise: At the end of each day, think back over the events of the day. Reflect on:

- What made you happy or proud?
- What challenges did you encounter and how did you respond?
- If you could redo one part of the day, what would it be and why?

Gratitude Reflection: At the end of each week, write down three things you were grateful for that week and why. Reflect on how acknowledging these things makes you feel.

These self-reflection exercises are designed to help you understand yourself better, recognize patterns in your thoughts and behaviors, and ultimately guide you toward more mindful living and decision-making.

The Importance of Self-Awareness: Next up, self-awareness. It's about knowing yourself – your strengths, weaknesses, what you want, and what scares you. It's understanding your values and passions, and what makes you, well, you. Self-awareness is key because it shows us what we need to work on and where we can grow.

We've included practical exercises to boost your self-awareness. These are designed to help you dig into your personal story, figure out what triggers your emotions, and identify your key strengths and areas for improvement. Writing down what you discover about yourself is a great way to get a clearer picture and start building a stronger sense of who you are.

Exploring self-reflection and self-awareness is an insightful journey into understanding yourself better. Here are exercises and techniques to help you dive deeper into these areas:

1. **Daily Reflection Journaling:** Start or end each day by writing in a journal. Focus on questions like:
2. What did I do well today?
3. What challenges did I face and how did I handle them?
4. What emotions did I feel today and why? Reflecting daily helps you notice patterns in your behavior and thoughts.
5. **The 'Why' Ladder:** For a particular behavior or feeling, keep asking yourself 'why' until you reach the root cause. For example, if you're upset about a work interaction, ask 'why' repeatedly to explore deeper reasons for your reaction.
6. **Value Assessment:** Write down your top five values and reflect on how these are (or aren't) reflected in your daily life. Think about times when you felt most aligned with these values and times when you didn't.
7. **Emotional Trigger Tracking:** Keep a log of moments when you felt a strong emotional reaction. Note the trigger, your response, and any patterns you notice. This can help identify what sets off certain emotions and how you might manage these reactions better.
8. **Strengths and Weaknesses Analysis:** Make two lists – one for strengths and one for weaknesses. Be honest with yourself. You can also ask trusted friends or family for their input. Understanding these can guide you in leveraging your strengths and addressing your weaknesses.
9. **Mindfulness and Meditation:** Regular mindfulness practice helps increase self-awareness. Spend a few minutes each day in quiet reflection or meditation, focusing on your thoughts, feelings, and bodily sensations.
10. **Life Timeline Activity:** Create a timeline of your life's major events, both positive and negative. Reflect on how these have

shaped you, what patterns emerge, and what you've learned from these experiences.

11. **Feedback Solicitation:** Actively ask for feedback from colleagues, friends, or family. This can provide an outside perspective on your strengths and areas for growth you might not be aware of.

12. **Role Model Reflection:** Think about people you admire or consider role models. What qualities do they have that you aspire to? How can you cultivate these qualities in yourself?

13. **Behavioral Experimentation:** Step out of your comfort zone by trying new activities or changing your routine. Observe how you react to these changes and what you learn about yourself.

14. **Skill-Development Plan:** Based on your strengths and weaknesses, develop a plan to enhance your skills. This could include taking courses, reading books, or seeking new experiences related to areas you want to improve.

By consistently engaging in these exercises, you'll gain deeper insights into your thoughts, feelings, and behaviors. This self-knowledge is a powerful tool for personal growth, resilience, and making more informed decisions in life.

Leveraging Your Strengths: Once you've got a good handle on your strengths, we'll show you how to use them to build up your resilience. Knowing your strengths helps you develop confidence and the skills to handle challenges.

To figure out your strengths, we suggest trying some self-assessment tests and getting feedback from people you trust. We also give you tips on how to use your strengths in different parts of your life – like in your relationships, at work, and when chasing your personal goals.

Leveraging your strengths effectively can significantly enhance various parts of your life. Here are examples of how to do this:

In the Workplace:

- If you have strong communication skills, you could volunteer to lead presentations or meetings.
- If you're good at organizing, offer to coordinate team projects or manage schedules.
- If problem-solving is your strength, tackle challenging tasks or propose solutions during brainstorming sessions.

In Personal Relationships:

- If empathy is one of your strengths, use it to build deeper connections by listening and being supportive in conversations with friends and family.
- If you're good at conflict resolution, you can help mediate issues among friends or family members.
- Use your sense of humor to lighten the mood in tense situations or to bond with others.

When Pursuing Personal Goals:

- If you're disciplined, apply this to setting and sticking to personal fitness or learning routines.
- If you're creative, channel this into hobbies like writing, painting, or crafting.
- For those who are good at planning, use this to outline and achieve long-term personal goals like saving for a house or planning a big trip.

In Community Involvement:

- If you have leadership skills, consider taking on a leadership role in a local community group or organizing community events.
- If you have teaching skills, volunteer to tutor students or conduct workshops in your area of expertise.
- If you're adept at fundraising or marketing, use these skills to support a cause you care about.

In Personal Development:

- If you're good at introspection, use this to continually assess and improve your life strategies.
- If you're resilient, use this strength to bounce back from setbacks in your personal or professional life.

In Networking:

- If you're outgoing and sociable, use these traits to network effectively and build professional relationships.
- If you have strong writing skills, leverage them to create impactful online profiles or to communicate effectively in professional networks.

In Financial Management:

- If you're good with numbers, apply this to managing your personal finances, investments, or budgeting.
- If you have a knack for research, use it to make informed decisions about financial opportunities or purchases.

In Education and Learning:

- If you excel in a particular subject, consider mentoring others in this area.
- If you're good at learning new languages, use this to broaden your cultural experiences or enhance your career opportunities.

By recognizing and applying your strengths in these different areas, you can improve your performance, increase your satisfaction, and make a more significant impact in both your personal and professional life. Remember, the key is to be aware of your strengths and actively seek opportunities where you can apply them.

. . .

By the end of this section, you'll clearly understand how important self-reflection and self-awareness are. Plus, you'll have solid strategies for figuring out your strengths. Armed with this knowledge, you're all set to build a solid foundation for resilience and face life's challenges with more confidence and strength.

THE POWER OF POSITIVE THINKING: BUILDING RESILIENCE THROUGH OPTIMISM

WHEN WE HIT A ROUGH PATCH, keeping a positive mindset can change the game. The power of positive thinking is a big help in building resilience and getting through challenges with a sense of grace and determination. In this section, we're looking at how staying positive affects our resilience and sharing tips on how to turn those negative thoughts around to a more optimistic viewpoint.

Resilience is all about bouncing back from tough times, setbacks, and challenges. You might think people are just naturally good at it, but resilience can be built up with the right mindset. Positive thinking is key here because it lets us face problems and setbacks with a sense of hope and optimism.

Shifting Negative Thoughts: The first step is tackling those negative thoughts we all get sometimes. It's normal to think negatively when we're dealing with hard stuff, but we have the power to change that. Changing negative thoughts means questioning them and flipping them into something positive and empowering.

For example, instead of seeing failure as a sign that you're not good enough, you can look at it as a chance to learn and grow. This shift in thinking helps us see setbacks as steps toward success. It also reminds us that obstacles aren't permanent – they're just hurdles we can get over with some persistence.

The Benefits of Positive Thinking: Staying positive helps boost our self-confidence and belief in ourselves, even when times are tough. When we're optimistic, we're more open to different solutions and see challenges as opportunities to grow and improve, not as things that hold us back.

To tap into positive thinking and grow our resilience, there are a few strategies we can use:

- **Mindfulness and Self-Awareness**: Being aware of our thoughts and feelings is important. When we catch ourselves thinking negatively, we can challenge those thoughts and replace them with something more positive.
- **Positive Affirmations and Gratitude**: Regularly practicing affirmations and gratitude can shift our mindset to be more optimistic.
- **Positive Influences and Support Networks**: Surrounding ourselves with positive people and building a supportive network is huge. Connecting with others who are optimistic and resilient can help keep our own mindset constructive, especially during tough times. Finding mentors or role models who show resilience and positivity can also be inspiring.

Wrapping it up, positive thinking is a powerful tool for building resilience in the face of adversity. By changing our negative thoughts and adopting an optimistic outlook, we turn challenges into opportunities for growth. Keeping a positive mindset not only strengthens our self-belief and confidence but also opens us up to new possibilities. Practicing mindfulness, using positive affirmations, and leaning on a supportive network are great ways to cultivate resilience and thrive through tough times.

~

BUILDING A STRONG SUPPORT NETWORK: NURTURING RESILIENCE THROUGH CONNECTION

INTRODUCTION: Resilience – that ability to adapt and bounce back from life's curveballs – doesn't just magically happen for most of us. It's something that can grow with the help of others. A strong support network is key for keeping up a resilient mindset and getting through tough times. This chapter is all about the power of a good support system and offers tips on building and strengthening your connections with family, friends, mentors, and colleagues.

Recognizing the Importance of a Support Network:

- **Psychological and emotional support**: It's comforting to have folks around who get what you're going through. They can be a source of comfort when things are rough.
- **Assistance and guidance**: A solid support network can offer practical help, advice, and a new way of looking at problems.

Building and Maintaining Relationships:

- **Family**: Make time for regular catch-ups and quality time with your family. Sharing your ups and downs helps build a trust-filled relationship.

- **Friends**: Invest in friendships that are supportive, dependable, and caring. Keep the lines of communication open and make time for each other.
- **Mentors**: Look for mentors who can give you solid advice and guidance, especially in tough situations. Their experience can be a real lifeline.
- **Colleagues**: Create a supportive atmosphere at work. Work together, help each other out, and build a work environment all about resilience.

Developing Effective Communication Skills:

- **Active listening**: Listen when others are talking about their struggles. They should feel heard and understood.
- **Expressing needs**: Be clear about what you need from others. It's all about giving and taking support.
- **Conflict resolution**: Learn how to handle disagreements in a way that's constructive. Keeping relationships strong even when there's a conflict is a big part of resilience.

Using Technology and Online Communities:

- **Virtual support networks**: Connect with online groups that share your interests. It's a great way to meet people dealing with similar things.
- **Social media boundaries**: Be smart about how you use social media. Focus on meaningful connections, and don't forget to set limits to protect your mental health.

Balancing Independence and Interdependence:

- **Cultivating self-reliance**: It's important to have a good support network, but handling things on your own is just as important.
- **Seeking support when needed**: Don't be afraid to ask for help. It's a strength, not a weakness, to know when you need a hand.

Conclusion: Resilience isn't something you're born with; it's something you can build, especially with the help of others. By creating strong connections with your family, friends, mentors, and colleagues, you're setting up a support network that can boost your resilience. Good communication, using technology wisely, and knowing when to be independent and when to lean on others are all part of building this network. So, start nurturing those relationships and watch how your resilience grows as you navigate through life's challenges.

PRACTICING SELF-CARE AND STRESS MANAGEMENT:

RESILIENCE IS all about bouncing back from tough spots and keeping on track. A big part of that resilience is handling stress well. When we're good at managing stress, we're setting ourselves up to face challenges head-on.

Self-Care Techniques for Stress Reduction and Resilience:

- **Regular Exercise**: Staying active is great for both your body and mind. It helps manage stress by releasing those feel-good endorphins. Find a workout you love – running, yoga, team sports – anything that gets you moving. Regular exercise can be a huge help in cutting down stress and boosting your resilience.
- **Meditation and Mindfulness**: Taking time to quiet your mind and focus on the now can lower your stress levels. Meditation and mindfulness are all about finding peace and calm within yourself. Try setting aside a few minutes each day to meditate. Find a quiet spot, focus on your breathing, or repeat a soothing phrase. Letting go of your worries and being present in the moment can work wonders for your stress and resilience.

- **Effective Time Management**: If you're always feeling rushed and behind, it can crank up your stress. Getting your time management in check – focusing on tasks, setting realistic goals, and making sure you have downtime – can help reduce stress and make life feel more balanced.
- **Supportive Relationships**: Having people around who support and encourage you is important for resilience. Keep in touch with family and friends, or maybe join a support group. Talking about what's on your mind can ease stress and make you feel more resilient.
- **Taking Breaks and Being Kind to Yourself**: It's okay to take a breather and do things you enjoy. Constantly pushing without rest can lead to burnout, which is a resilience killer. Set aside time for your favorite activities, like reading, music, or hobbies. And be kind to yourself – acknowledge the good things you do instead of being too hard on yourself.

Building resilience doesn't happen overnight. It's a process that takes time and effort. By weaving these self-care techniques into your life, you can lower your stress levels, strengthen your resilience, and be better prepared to tackle life's challenges.

EMBRACING FAILURE AND LEARNING FROM SETBACKS:

SOMETIMES LIFE THROWS US CURVEBALLS – obstacles, setbacks, and failures that can knock the wind out of our sails. It's easy to feel down and scared to try again, fearing we might mess up. But here's the thing: failure isn't the end of the road. It's actually a steppingstone toward resilience and personal growth. In this chapter, we're all about turning a growth mindset on and learning to see failure as a chance to learn, develop, and set ourselves up for success down the line.

Reframing Failure:

- **A New Perspective on Failure**: Remember, failure is just part of life. What matters is how you look at it and what you do after. Instead of seeing it as a roadblock, think of it as a learning opportunity. With a growth mindset, you see failures as chances to grow. This shift in thinking helps us focus on what we can learn from the experience, rather than feeling bummed about it.

Overcoming Fear and Embracing Mistakes:

- **Taking on Fear**: The fear of failing can hold us back. We worry about messing up and what others might think. But this chapter will show you ways to get past that fear. It's about seeing mistakes as part of the process of improving and growing. When we create a safe space for errors, we open ourselves up to new ideas and opportunities.

Learning from Failure:

- **Turning Setbacks into Lessons**: Failure doesn't mean you're out of the game. It's actually a chance to learn and pick up some valuable insights. We'll talk about how to reflect on what went wrong, spot areas for improvement, and pick up new skills. Self-reflection can reveal a lot about our strengths and weaknesses and help us make smarter choices.

Building Resilience:

- **Bouncing Back Stronger**: Embracing failure and learning from it is a huge part of building resilience. We'll explore ways to strengthen your resilience, like keeping a positive mindset, taking care of yourself, finding support, and setting realistic goals. Resilience is about adapting and using failures as fuel for growth and success.

Conclusion: Failure isn't a sign of your worth or your potential; it's a part of your journey. This chapter is about teaching you to look at failures as opportunities for growth. We'll show you how to reframe setbacks, embrace your mistakes, and use them as a springboard for success in all areas of your life. So, let's get ready to learn from our stumbles and grow stronger from them!

DEVELOPING PROBLEM-SOLVING SKILLS:

RESILIENCE IS like your personal toolkit for getting through life's rough patches. An important tool in there? Problem-solving. It's all about figuring out the best ways to tackle obstacles and come up with smart solutions.

Critical Thinking: Your Problem-Solving Secret Weapon:

- **Think It Through**: Critical thinking is huge when solving problems. It's about looking at a situation, digging into what's going on, and weighing your options. By using critical thinking, you approach problems in a structured, logical way, helping you make choices based on solid info.

Brainstorming: Unleashing Your Creative Side:

- **Let the Ideas Flow**: Brainstorming is another killer strategy for problem-solving. It's when you let your ideas run wild and come up with many solutions, without worrying about how good or bad they are. This open, free-wheeling thinking can lead you to some innovative answers you might not have thought of otherwise.

Seeking Outside Perspectives: A Fresh Take on Problems:

- **Get a Different View**: When you're deep in a problem, it's easy to get tunnel vision. That's why getting opinions from others can be a game-changer. Talking to different people can give you new insights, other ways of looking at things, and solutions you might not have seen before.

Adaptability and Flexibility: Rolling with the Punches:

- **Stay Open and Ready to Change**: Being adaptable and flexible is key in problem-solving. Life can throw curveballs and shifting your approach or thinking of a plan B (or C or D) keeps you on your toes and ready for anything. It's about being open to different solutions, even if they're not what you first had in mind.

Developing your problem-solving skills is a big part of strengthening your resilience. By improving at critical thinking, brainstorming, seeking different perspectives, and staying adaptable, you're gearing up to face challenges head-on. These skills don't just help you find solutions; they give you the confidence to tackle problems and bounce back stronger from any setbacks.

SECTION FOUR WRAP-UP:

KEY POINTS:

Understanding the Concept of Resilience

- **Emotional Regulation:** The ability to manage and cope with negative emotions.
- **Problem Solving and Decision Making:** Thinking through problems creatively and making informed choices.
- **Impact on Relationships and Social Interactions:** Strengthening connections and handling conflicts effectively.
- **Personal Growth and Development:** Embracing failures and setbacks as opportunities for learning and self-improvement.

Identifying Personal Strengths and Weaknesses

- **Understanding Self-Reflection:** Analyzing thoughts, feelings, and actions for better decision-making.
- **Importance of Self-Awareness:** Knowing personal strengths, weaknesses, and values for growth.

- **Leveraging Your Strengths:** Using personal strengths in various parts of life for improvement and success.

The Power of Positive Thinking

- **Influence of Mindset:** The role of a positive outlook in overcoming challenges.
- **Reframing Challenges:** Viewing difficulties as opportunities rather than obstacles.
- **Benefits of Positive Thinking:** Enhancing problem-solving skills and resilience through optimism.

Building a Strong Support Network

- **Importance of Support:** Emotional, psychological, and practical benefits of a support system.
- **Developing Effective Communication Skills:** Improving relationships through active listening and clear expression of needs.
- **Using Technology and Online Communities:** Leveraging virtual support for more perspectives and resources.

Practicing Self-Care and Stress Management

- **Self-Care Techniques:** using methods like exercise and meditation for stress reduction.
- **Impact of Personal Challenges:** Understanding how personal issues can affect professional life and overall happiness.

Embracing Failure and Learning from Setbacks

- **Reframing Failure:** Changing perspectives to see failure as a learning opportunity.
- **Overcoming Fear:** Addressing the fear of failure to embrace mistakes and grow.

Developing Problem-Solving Skills

- **Critical Thinking:** using logical analysis for effective problem-solving.
- **Brainstorming:** Encouraging creativity in finding solutions.
- **Adaptability and Flexibility:** Remaining open to changing approaches and new ideas.

ACTION ITEMS:

To Develop Resilience

- **Practice Emotional Regulation:** Engage in activities like meditation to improve emotional control.
- **Enhance Problem-Solving Skills:** Regularly challenge yourself with new problems to think creatively.
- **Strengthen Relationships:** Communicate effectively and build a supportive network.
- **Focus on Personal Development:** Set goals for learning and self-improvement.

To Identify Strengths and Weaknesses

- **Regular Self-Reflection:** Journal daily to uncover patterns in behavior and thinking.
- **Engage in Self-Awareness Exercises:** Conduct a personal SWOT analysis and seek feedback.
- **Apply Strengths in Life:** Utilize identified strengths in professional and personal settings.

To Cultivate a Positive Mindset

- **Practice Positive Affirmations:** Daily affirmations to reinforce optimism.
- **Engage in Mindfulness:** Incorporate mindfulness practices to maintain a positive outlook.

- **Surround Yourself with Positivity:** Choose relationships and environments that foster positive thinking.

To Build a Support Network

- **Foster Strong Relationships:** Actively maintain and nurture connections with family and friends.
- **Develop Communication Skills:** Practice active listening and clear expression in interactions.
- **Leverage Online Communities:** Join forums and groups for more support and perspectives.

For Effective Self-Care and Stress Management

- **Implement Self-Care Routines:** Schedule regular physical activities and relaxation techniques.
- **Balance Professional and Personal Life:** Set boundaries and manage time efficiently to reduce stress.

To Embrace Failure

- **Reframe Perspective on Failure:** Shift mindset to view setbacks as learning opportunities.
- **Challenge Fear of Failure:** Take risks and learn from the outcomes, despite success or failure.

To Enhance Problem-Solving Skills

- **Engage in Critical Thinking Exercises:** Regularly practice logical thinking and analysis.
- **Brainstorm Creatively:** Set aside time for unrestricted idea generation.
- **Adapt and Flex:** Be open to changing strategies and exploring various solutions.

In Our Next Section:

In our next section, we delve into the transformative power of resilience in the face of life's unpredictable twists and turns. As we journey through this exploration, remember that resilience isn't just about weathering storms—it's about emerging stronger, more adaptable, and more self-aware. We'll unpack the essential tools and mindsets that transform challenges into steppingstones for growth. Imagine turning every setback into a setup for a comeback, where each difficulty is an opportunity to learn, grow, and redefine your path.

Get ready to embrace a journey of self-discovery, where you'll learn not just to survive, but to thrive amidst life's complexities. We'll be diving into practical strategies to enhance your resilience, from cultivating a growth mindset to developing strong problem-solving skills. This journey is about more than just overcoming obstacles; it's about building a life where you're constantly evolving, learning, and moving forward with confidence and purpose. So, gear up for an empowering exploration that will equip you with the resilience to turn life's challenges into your greatest victories.

SECTION FIVE: BUILDING A SUPPORT NETWORK

IMPORTANCE OF BUILDING A SUPPORT NETWORK FOR PERSONAL AND PROFESSIONAL DEVELOPMENT

BUILDING a solid support network is important for both your personal and professional growth. It's like having a team behind you, providing the guidance, encouragement, and resources you need to tackle challenges and hit your goals. Here's a breakdown of why having a support network is a game-changer:

- **Emotional Support**: When times are tough, having people who get what you're going through can make a world of difference. Talking about your challenges and getting advice or encouragement from folks who care can help you manage those tricky situations. This support keeps you motivated and resilient, which is key for growing personally and professionally.
- **Different Perspectives**: A support network brings together people from many backgrounds, offering you a wealth of perspectives, ideas, and experiences. Hanging out with a diverse group opens up your mind to new ways of thinking, solving problems, and getting creative. You can learn so much from others' experiences, which is great for your professional development.

- **Skill Development**: With a support network, you have access to mentorship and professional groups where you can learn new skills and techniques. Learning from people who've been where you want to go can speed up your own development.
- **Accountability**: Sharing your goals with your support network creates a sense of responsibility to follow through. They can help keep you on track, remind you of your commitments, and provide that little nudge you need sometimes. This accountability is a powerful motivator for growth.
- **Networking and Collaboration**: A support network opens doors to new networking opportunities and potential collaborations. Connecting with people who share your interests or goals can lead to exciting projects and partnerships. Working together not only helps your professional development but also lets you share knowledge and resources.
- **Boosting Confidence and Self-esteem**: Being surrounded by positive, supportive people can boost your confidence and belief in your abilities. This environment encourages you to take risks and try new things, which is so important for personal and professional growth.
- **Resilience and Motivation**: When you hit a roadblock, a strong support network can give you the push you need to keep going. Having cheerleaders in your corner can boost your determination and resilience. They help you stay focused on your goals and keep moving forward.

Having a support network is important for your growth, both personally and professionally. It gives everything from emotional backing and new perspectives to skill-building, accountability, networking opportunities, confidence boosts, and the motivation to keep going. By surrounding yourself with the right people, you're setting yourself up for a successful and fulfilling life.

IDENTIFYING THE RIGHT INDIVIDUALS TO INCLUDE IN YOUR SUPPORT NETWORK

WHEN YOU'RE BUILDING your support network, it's important to pick the right folks. This network is your go-to for emotional support, advice, and a helping hand when you need it. Getting the right people on board can make a difference in reaching your goals and tackling challenges. Here are pointers on finding the right people for your support network:

- **Define Your Needs**: First things first, figure out what you need help with. Looking for career advice, someone to listen when times are tough, or help with a project? Knowing what you need helps you figure out who to look for.
- **Different Roles for Different Needs**: Your support network can have people who play various roles. Maybe you need a mentor for advice, friends for emotional support, or colleagues who can open doors professionally. Think about what roles will be most helpful for your growth.
- **Look at Who You Already Know**: Check out your current circle – friends, coworkers, acquaintances. Some might already be supportive in different ways. Maybe it's time to strengthen those relationships more.

- **Finding Like-Minded People**: It's great to connect with people who share your interests or goals. It can give you a sense of belonging and mutual understanding. Look for communities or groups that line up with what you're passionate about.
- **Compatibility Matters**: Think about personalities and values. You want to be around people who lift you up and make you feel comfortable, especially when you're sharing both the good and the tough stuff.
- **Embrace Diversity**: While it's awesome to have people who 'get' you, diversity in your network is key too. Folks from different backgrounds can offer new perspectives and ideas you might not have considered.
- **Reliability Is Key**: Choose people who are actually there when you need them. Think about how willing they are to listen and help, and whether they've been dependable in the past.
- **Quality Over Quantity**: It's not about having a huge network. It's about having the right people – those who genuinely care and are invested in your success.

Building a support network doesn't happen overnight. It takes time and effort, and it's something you'll probably tweak as you go along. Regularly check in on your network to make sure it's still meeting your needs and be open to adding new faces as your goals and life change.

STRATEGIES FOR NURTURING AND MAINTAINING RELATIONSHIPS WITHIN YOUR SUPPORT NETWORK

MAINTAINING HEALTHY, meaningful relationships in your support network is a big deal for your personal growth and well-being. Here are strategies to help you keep these connections strong and thriving:

- **Open and Honest Communication**: Communication is key in any relationship. Be clear, honest, and open. Share your thoughts, feelings, and worries with your network and encourage them to do the same. This builds trust and understanding.
- **Active Listening**: Listen to what others are saying. Pay full attention, make eye contact, and respond thoughtfully. This makes people feel valued and understood.
- **Show Empathy**: Empathy is all about feeling what others feel. Try to understand things from their perspective. Be compassionate, confirm their emotions, and be there for them. This strengthens your bonds.
- **Be Reliable and Trustworthy**: Trust is built over time. Be someone your network can rely on. Stick to your commitments, be dependable, and handle your responsibilities. Trust is the foundation of solid relationships.

- **Offer Support**: Be there for your support network when they need it. Help out, listen, or just check in on them. Show you care and provide encouragement. Your support makes your connections stronger and more reciprocal.
- **Respect Boundaries**: Everyone has their own limits. Respect these and don't push people past their comfort zone. Be aware of personal space, emotional needs, and time commitments. Understanding boundaries makes for healthier relationships.
- **Celebrate Successes**: Cheer on the successes of your support network. Be genuinely happy for them and congratulate them on their wins, big or small. Celebrating together strengthens your bond and creates a positive vibe.
- **Resolve Conflicts Constructively**: Conflicts happen, but it's how you handle them that matters. Be open-minded and humble when disagreements pop up. Avoid blaming or getting defensive. Focus on understanding each other and finding a solution that works for both sides.
- **Be Present and Available**: When you're with your support network, be all there – physically, mentally, and emotionally. Avoid distractions and make quality time a priority. Doing activities together, like regular meet-ups or shared hobbies, helps deepen your relationships.
- **Appreciate and Express Gratitude**: Show your gratitude to those in your support network. Acknowledge their help, kindness, and impact on your life. A sincere thank you goes a long way in showing they're valued and appreciated.

Remember, keeping up relationships is a two-way street that needs effort and commitment. By putting these strategies into practice, you can nurture and maintain strong, fulfilling connections with the people who support you.

HOW TO LEVERAGE YOUR SUPPORT NETWORK FOR ADVICE, GUIDANCE, AND RESOURCES

LEVERAGING your support network for advice, guidance, and resources can be a real boost in both your personal and professional worlds. Think about it: you have friends, family, colleagues, mentors, and other connections who can offer their insights, contacts, and know-how. Here's how to make the most of that network:

- **Identify Who's Who**: First, figure out who in your life could offer the advice, guidance, or resources you need. Who's got the experience or connections that could help you out? This could be anyone from family members to old coworkers, mentors, people in your field, or even folks you connect with online.
- **Build Strong Relationships**: Keep those connections strong. Stay in touch through calls, emails, or meet-ups. Show you're interested in them, too, and offer support when they need it. Stronger relationships mean it's easier to ask for and get help when you need it.
- **Be Clear About What You Need**: When you ask for help, be specific. Instead of vague requests, pinpoint exactly what you're looking for. It saves time and makes it easier for people

to give you the right help. For example, instead of a broad "Can you help with my career?", try "Do you have insights into marketing careers or know someone who does?"

- **Reach Out for Advice and Guidance**: When you're up against something tough, need to decide, or want insight on a topic, tap into your network. Set up a time to talk it out. Be open to your thoughts and ready to listen to what they have to say.
- **Use Their Skills and Resources**: If someone in your network has skills or resources you need, please ask for help. Maybe they can look over your resume, give feedback on a project, or help you learn a new skill. They might also know about books, courses, or events that could be just what you need.
- **Show Your Appreciation and Give Back**: Always say thanks for any help you get. Let them know you appreciate their time and effort. And look for ways to return the favor. It could be sharing your own skills or making a connection that could help them out. This give-and-take makes your network even stronger.
- **Keep Growing Your Network**: Always be on the lookout for new connections. Go to industry events, join professional groups, get involved in online communities, or attend workshops. Expanding your network brings new perspectives and more resources.

Your support network is a fantastic resource for your growth. By nurturing those relationships, asking for help when you need it, and being there for them in return, you can make the most of your network for advice, guidance, and resources.

~

BUILDING A DIVERSE SUPPORT NETWORK TO GAIN DIFFERENT PERSPECTIVES AND INSIGHTS

BUILDING a diverse support network is essential for getting different points of view and insights. When you're around people from various backgrounds, with different experiences and thoughts, you open yourself up to learning so much more. This variety of views can bring new ideas to the table, challenge what you think you know, and give you a fuller perspective on many topics. Here's how you can create a diverse support network:

- **Figure Out What You Want to Learn**: Start by thinking about what areas in your life or career you want more insight into. Maybe there's a specific industry or skill set you're curious about.
- **Find the Right People and Groups**: Dive into finding people or groups who know their stuff in the areas you're interested in. Use social media, online communities, professional networks, and local organizations to connect with these folks.
- **Get Out There and Join Communities**: Go to networking events, sign up for professional groups, or go to conferences. Places like these are perfect for meeting people who share your

interests and can offer new perspectives. Be open to chatting with new people and getting to know them.

- **Look for Different Perspectives**: It's comfortable to stick with people who think like you but try to push past that. Contact people from different walks of life, with diverse cultures and viewpoints. This could mean joining groups that focus on diversity or seeking mentorship from someone with a unique take on things.
- **Build Real Relationships**: A support network isn't just about having a bunch of contacts. It's about forming real, meaningful relationships based on trust and mutual respect. Get to know people on a deeper level.
- **Encourage Open, Inclusive Communication**: Make sure your network is a place where everyone feels comfortable sharing their ideas and experiences. Listen actively and engage in discussions that let everyone learn from each other.
- **Keep the Network Alive**: Building your network is an ongoing thing. Stay involved by going to events, joining in on discussions, and keeping in regular contact. And remember, networking is a give-and-take – be ready to offer your own support and help too.

Building a diverse support network doesn't happen overnight. Be patient, keep an open mind, and stay committed. Enjoy the richness that comes from all these different perspectives and experiences and watch how they broaden your own understanding and knowledge.

BALANCING GIVING AND RECEIVING SUPPORT WITHIN YOUR NETWORK

BALANCING GIVING and receiving support in your network is key to keeping your relationships healthy and fostering a space where everyone supports each other. Here's how you can strike that balance:

- **Know What You Need**: Start by figuring out what kind of support you're looking for, whether it's emotional, practical, or career-related. Knowing what you need helps you communicate more clearly and genuinely with your network.
- **Set Your Boundaries**: It's important to set boundaries so you don't feel drained or overwhelmed. Be clear about what you can give and what you're hoping to get back. Share these boundaries openly with your network.
- **Give Support Wholeheartedly**: When you're helping someone out, do it with real care and attention. Listen to their needs with empathy. This helps build a network that's supportive on both sides.
- **Don't Be Shy to Ask for Help**: If you need support, just ask. It's not a sign of weakness; it's actually brave. Contact friends, family, or colleagues you trust for the guidance or help you need.

- **Practice Give and Take**: It's all about give and take. When someone offers you help, accept it and show your gratitude. This lets them know they're valued and keeps the spirit of mutual support alive.
- **Keep Things Balanced**: Try to keep a good balance between helping others and looking after your own needs. If you feel like you're giving too much or not getting enough support, it might be time to reassess and adjust.
- **Be an Active Networker**: Stay actively involved with your network. Show interest in others, offer help, and respond to their needs. By taking the lead, you encourage a culture of mutual support.
- **Communicate Clearly**: Keep the lines of communication open and honest. If you're feeling swamped and can't offer support, say so. And if you're the one needing support, be clear about what would help you the most.

Balancing support is something you'll be working on continuously. It involves participating actively, communicating well, and being genuine with your network. By keeping this balance, you're building relationships beneficial for everyone, helping with growth, resilience, and overall well-being.

THE POWER OF RECIPROCITY AND SUPPORTING OTHERS IN YOUR NETWORK

THE POWER of reciprocity and supporting others in your network is a huge deal. This give-and-take principle is what makes relationships meaningful, builds trust, and paves the way for everyone to succeed. Reciprocity is all about helping each other out, and in a professional setting, this can create an environment where everyone's thriving.

- **Building Goodwill**: When you're there for others in your network, like giving advice, sharing resources, or lending a hand, you're laying down a foundation of goodwill. This not only strengthens your ties but also encourages others to give back. It's about creating a network where everyone's got each other's back.
- **The Benefits of Helping Out**: Supporting your network is a win-win. You get known as someone reliable and trustworthy. Being that go-to person who helps expecting nothing in return can draw people to you. This could open up many doors, like new collaborations or opportunities you wouldn't have found otherwise.
- **Creating a Ripple Effect**: Helping someone often inspires them to help others too. It's like starting a positive chain

reaction. This builds a culture where everyone's supporting each other, and the whole network benefits. It lifts everyone's chances of success.

- **Be Genuine**: It's important to be authentic when you're helping out. It's not about keeping score or waiting for payback. It's more about genuinely wanting to see others succeed. People can tell when you're sincere, and that's when reciprocity takes off.

To wrap it up, the impact of reciprocity and being there for others in your network is massive. By giving and receiving support, you're not only beefing up your relationships but also creating a setup where everyone can do well. So go ahead, invest in your network, be generous with your support, and you'll see how it comes back to you.

SECTION FIVE WRAP-UP:

- **Emotional Support**: Having a network for emotional backing during tough times.
- **Diverse Perspectives**: Access to varied ideas and experiences from different backgrounds.
- **Skill Development**: Learning new skills and techniques from your network.
- **Accountability**: Sharing goals for mutual encouragement and accountability.
- **Networking and Collaboration**: Opening doors to new opportunities and partnerships.
- **Confidence and Self-Esteem**: Support network boosts confidence and self-belief.
- **Resilience and Motivation**: Support networks provide motivation and help maintain focus.
- **Identifying Needs**: Understanding your own needs to find suitable support.
- **Varied Roles**: Different people in the network can fulfill different support roles.

- **Existing Relationships**: Leveraging existing relationships in your circle.
- **Like-Minded Individuals**: Seeking people with shared interests or goals.
- **Reliability and Quality**: Prioritizing dependable and meaningful connections.
- **Communication and Listening**: Importance of clear communication and active listening.
- **Empathy**: Showing understanding and compassion within the network.
- **Trust and Reliability**: Being a trustworthy and reliable member of the network.
- **Support and Assistance**: Being available to offer and accept support.
- **Respecting Boundaries**: Acknowledging and respecting personal limits.
- **Celebrating Successes**: Sharing and celebrating each other's achievements.
- **Conflict Resolution**: Handling disagreements constructively.
- **Presence and Availability**: Being present and accessible in interactions.
- **Gratitude**: Expressing appreciation for the support received.
- **Advice, Guidance, and Resources**: Utilizing your network for diverse support.
- **Building Relationships**: Strengthening connections for effective support.
- **Clarity of Needs**: Clearly communicating what help you need.
- **Diverse Network**: Building a network with varied backgrounds for broader perspectives.
- **Active Networking**: Continuously engaging and growing your network.
- **Balancing Support**: Maintaining a healthy give-and-take in relationships.
- **Reciprocity**: Understanding the importance of mutual support and help.

ACTION ITEMS:

- **Evaluate Your Needs**: Assess the type of support you need for personal and professional growth.
- **Cultivate Existing Relationships**: Strengthen connections with people you already know.
- **Expand Your Network**: Join groups or communities related to your interests to meet like-minded individuals.
- **Be Open and Honest**: Communicate your thoughts and needs clearly to your network.
- **Practice Active Listening**: Pay attention and show empathy in your interactions.
- **Provide Reliable Support**: Be dependable and trustworthy in your commitments.
- **Set and Respect Boundaries**: Clearly define and respect personal and professional limits.
- **Celebrate and Acknowledge**: Recognize and celebrate the successes of your network members.
- **Resolve Conflicts Constructively**: Approach disagreements with an open mind and aim for resolution.
- **Stay Present and Engaged**: Be engaged and present during interactions.
- **Express Gratitude**: Show appreciation for the support and help you receive.
- **Identify Key Individuals**: Determine who in your network can provide specific advice or resources.
- **Request Specific Help**: Be clear about the assistance or guidance you need.
- **Give Back**: Offer your support and resources to others in your network.
- **Balance Giving and Receiving**: Ensure a healthy balance of support within your relationships.
- **Seek Diverse Perspectives**: Actively look for people with different backgrounds and experiences.
- **Nurture Your Network**: Regularly engage with your network to maintain strong connections.

- **Reflect on Reciprocity**: Recognize the mutual benefits of supporting others in your network.
- **Actively Support Others**: Offer help and guidance to members of your network when needed.
- **Monitor Your Network's Dynamics**: Regularly assess the effectiveness and dynamics of your support network.

In Our Next Section:

In our next section, we'll start a journey to harness the transformative power of resilience in the face of adversity. Life, with all its unpredictable twists and turns, often tests our fortitude and adaptability. But within each of us lies an incredible strength waiting to be unlocked. This section will guide you in nurturing that inner resilience, helping you to not only withstand life's storms but to emerge from them stronger and more capable. We'll explore practical, actionable strategies that empower you to turn obstacles into steppingstones, fostering a mindset that views challenges not as insurmountable walls, but as opportunities for growth and self-discovery.

Get ready to dig into a world where resilience becomes your most trusted ally. We'll give you the tools and insights necessary to build a resilient spirit, one that embraces change, learns from setbacks, and finds strength in vulnerability. You'll discover how to maintain a positive outlook, even in the face of daunting challenges, and how to tap into the power of a supportive community. This journey is about transforming your approach to life's hurdles, making sure with each challenge you face, you grow wiser, stronger, and more equipped to handle whatever comes next. Let's start this path of resilience together, ready to face life's challenges with confidence and grace.

SECTION SIX: PROBLEM-SOLVING TECHNIQUES FOR OVERCOMING CHALLENGES

INTRODUCTION TO PROBLEM-SOLVING TECHNIQUES:

THIS SECTION IS all about problem-solving skills – a valuable tool in your kit for tackling life's challenges. In a world full of obstacles, being a great problem solver sets you apart.

- **Why Problem-Solving Skills Matter**: Developing strong problem-solving skills does more than just help you get past difficulties. It sharpens your decision-making abilities, hones your critical thinking, and boosts your overall confidence. Whether it's in your personal life or at work, facing problems head-on is key for growth and success.
- **Systematic Approaches to Problem-Solving**: To solve problems effectively, you need a structured approach. We will dive into several techniques that help break down problems and find solid solutions. For example, there's the 5-Whys technique, where you ask "why" five times to drill down to the root of a problem. Getting to the heart of the issue means you can come up with targeted solutions.
- **Fishbone Diagrams**: Another tool we'll explore is the fishbone diagram, or Ishikawa diagram. This helps you visually map out different categories that might be causing a problem. By

looking closely at each category, you can pinpoint likely causes and come up with good solutions.

- **Brainstorming for Creative Solutions**: We'll also talk about brainstorming. This technique is all about letting the ideas flow, working together, and considering many possibilities before zeroing in on the best solutions. It's a great way to spark creativity and collaborative thinking.
- **Using a Decision Matrix**: Another technique covered is the decision matrix. This involves evaluating different solutions against a set of criteria and assigning weights to each. It's a fantastic way to objectively compare options and focus on the ones that align best with what you're aiming for.
- **The Role of Feedback and Reflection**: Finally, we'll highlight the importance of feedback and reflection in problem-solving. Evaluating how effective your solutions are and learning from experiences is important for getting better at handling challenges. Feedback helps fine-tune your problem-solving approach for future challenges.

To wrap it up, this section is all about why problem-solving skills are so important and how you can use different techniques to tackle problems effectively. By building up these skills and using these strategies, you can approach problems with more confidence, creativity, and effectiveness, leading to success in all areas of your life.

THE PROBLEM-SOLVING PROCESS:

PROBLEM-SOLVING IS a handy skill that comes into play in many situations, whether you're dealing with personal stuff or professional challenges. It's all about figuring out what the issue is and then working through a structured process to solve it. Let's walk through the steps involved in problem-solving and talk about why having a systematic approach matters.

- **Define the Problem**: First up, you've got to get a clear handle on the problem. This means pinpointing exactly what's going wrong, figuring out why it's happening, and understanding what you're aiming to achieve by solving it. When you've got a clear definition of the problem, you can focus all your energy on finding the right solution.
- **Gather Information**: Once you know what you're dealing with, gather all the info you can about the issue. Look up relevant facts, collect data, and chat with people who might have useful insights. The more information you have, the better you'll understand the problem and the different ways you could solve it.

- **Generate Alternative Solutions**: Now it's time to brainstorm. Think up as many solutions as you can. You could use mind maps, list out pros and cons, or even have a group discussion to get those ideas flowing. The key here is to be creative and open to many possibilities.
- **Evaluate Options**: With a bunch of potential solutions on the table, start weighing them up. Look at the pros and cons of each, think about how feasible they are, and consider what risks or benefits they might bring. This step helps you narrow down your options to the ones most likely to work.
- **Implement the Chosen Solution**: Got a solution picked out? Great – now it's time to make it happen. Work out a plan for how you'll implement it, decide who's going to do what, and sort out any resources you need. Make sure everyone involved knows the plan and is on board. Then, get started and keep an eye on how things are going.

By following these steps, problem-solving becomes a neat, orderly process. It keeps you from making snap decisions, makes sure you've considered everything important, and ups your chances of coming up with a solution that works.

Wrapping it up, problem-solving is a skill you can get better at with some practice. By sticking to this systematic approach – defining the problem, gathering info, brainstorming solutions, evaluating your options, and then putting your plan into action – you'll be well on your way to becoming a top-notch problem solver. This methodical way of tackling issues helps you analyze the problem thoroughly, sparks more creative solutions, and generally leads to better outcomes.

BRAINSTORMING AND CREATIVE THINKING:

BRAINSTORMING: **Letting Ideas Flow**:

- **Brainstorming Basics**: This technique is all about coming up with lots of ideas really quickly, without worrying about if they're good or not. It's a free-thinking, judgment-free zone that gets the creative juices flowing.

Mind Mapping: Visualizing Thoughts:

- **Making Connections with Mind Maps**: Mind mapping is a visual way to organize your ideas. You start with a central idea and then branch out into related thoughts, creating a web of connections. It's great for creative thinking because it lets you see new links and possibilities.

Overcoming Creative Roadblocks:

- **Busting Through Barriers**: Common creativity stoppers include fear of messing up, doubting yourself, and getting stuck in the same old thinking patterns. To get past these, try to stay positive and open-minded, embrace the unknown, and question your assumptions. Creating a space where it's okay to take risks and try new things can also help unleash your creative potential.

Diverse Perspectives and Teamwork:

- **Mixing It Up for More Ideas**: Collaborating with people from different backgrounds can kick your creativity into high gear. Getting input from colleagues, stakeholders, or online groups can spark some innovative solutions. Teamwork is great for challenging old ideas and coming up with new ones through shared brainpower.

Try, Test, and Evolve:

- **The Power of Experimentation**: Creative thinking often means trying out new ideas and tweaking them as you go. Test your ideas, build prototypes, get feedback, and refine your ideas. Adopting a "try fast, learn fast" approach can lead to some amazing breakthroughs and continuous improvement.

Setting the Scene for Creativity:

- **Your Environment Matters**: Believe it or not, where you are can affect how creative you are. A workspace that's stimulating and inspiring, with all the resources and tools you need, can encourage creative thinking. Also, giving yourself time to think, be alone, or relax can spark great ideas.

Keep Learning and Stay Curious:

- **Curiosity Leads to Creativity**: Keeping your mind open and always learning new things can do wonders for your creativity.

Stay up to date with what's happening in your field, check out workshops or conferences, and even explore hobbies or activities outside work. These things can open up new perspectives and inspire fresh ideas.

CRITICAL THINKING AND ANALYTICAL SKILLS:

IN THIS PART, we're diving into how critical thinking is valuable when solving problems. It's all about tackling challenges with a clear, logical head, which leads to smarter decisions and better outcomes.

- **Objective Analysis**: A big part of critical thinking is looking at info objectively. That means checking out the facts and evidence without letting your own biases get in the way. When you can critically analyze stuff, you get a deeper understanding of the problem and come up with well-informed solutions.
- **Spotting Patterns**: Another cool skill in critical thinking is pattern recognition. A lot of problems have certain trends or patterns. If you can spot these, you get a better handle on the problem and can come up with effective ways to deal with it. Plus, recognizing patterns can help you see future challenges coming and prepare ahead of time.
- **Evaluating Sources**: In our world where info is everywhere, it's important to figure out what's credible and what's not. Critical thinking involves checking out how valid and reliable

your sources are. You want to make sure the info you're using is accurate, relevant, and comes from someone trustworthy.

Ways to Boost Your Critical Thinking Skills:

- **Reflective Thinking**: Regularly take time to think about your own thinking. Understanding your assumptions and biases helps you get better at approaching problems more objectively.
- **Ask Deeper Questions**: Push yourself to think deeper by asking questions that make you analyze information. This helps uncover patterns or connections that aren't immediately obvious.
- **Seek Different Views**: When you're tackling a problem, try to get input from a variety of people. Different perspectives can challenge your own views and broaden your understanding.
- **Critically Evaluate Information**: Make a habit of critically looking at the info you come across. Focus on sources that are credible and well-supported by evidence. This helps you tell apart reliable information from stuff that's not so trustworthy.
- **Logical Reasoning**: Use logical reasoning to make sense of information and form sound judgments. This involves evaluating evidence, thinking about cause-and-effect, and spotting any flaws in arguments.

Wrapping it up, critical thinking is a key player in problem-solving. It's about objectively analyzing info, recognizing patterns, and evaluating sources to come up with effective solutions. By working on your critical thinking skills – reflecting on your thoughts, asking the right questions, embracing diverse viewpoints, evaluating info, and applying logic – you can sharpen your problem-solving abilities and make smart choices in all areas of life.

DECISION-MAKING TECHNIQUES:

W<small>HEN WE'RE CONSTANTLY FACING</small> tough calls, whether it's picking the right investment or figuring out the best move in a crisis, having solid decision-making techniques up your sleeve is key. Let's dive into some methods that can help you tackle challenges and make smart choices.

The Decision Matrix: A Structured Approach:

- **How It Works**: The decision matrix is like a tool that helps you break down complex choices. You list out your options and the factors that matter for your decision, assigning a weight to each factor based on how important it is. Then, you rate each option against these criteria and work out a score. The option with the highest score usually gets the green light. This method is great for sorting through complicated decisions methodically.

Cost-Benefit Analysis: Weighing Pros and Cons:

- **Balancing Costs and Benefits**: Here, you compare the costs of a decision (like money, time, effort) against what you'll gain from it (like profits, efficiency, market share). Putting numbers to these factors helps you see which option gives you the most bang for your buck.

SWOT Analysis: Strategic Thinking:

- **Looking at All Angles**: SWOT analysis gets you to look at strengths, weaknesses, opportunities, and threats related to your decision. This way, you consider both what's working in your favor and what's not, plus what external factors might help or hinder you. It's a thorough way to scope out the whole situation before you decide.

Other Considerations:

- **Context and Information**: Don't forget to think about the bigger picture. Gather all the relevant info and chat with people who might be affected by the decision or have insights to share. A well-rounded approach helps you avoid biases and base your decision on solid info.

To wrap it up, techniques like the decision matrix, cost-benefit analysis, and SWOT analysis are useful for navigating complex challenges and making informed decisions. By breaking things down, weighing up costs and benefits, and considering all the internal and external factors, you can boost your chances of making a decision that leads to the results you're after.

EFFECTIVE COMMUNICATION AND COLLABORATION:

WHEN YOU'RE TRYING to solve problems, being good at communication is a game changer. It lets people swap info, ideas, and viewpoints, which all help in making smarter decisions and finding the best solutions.

Active Listening: A Cornerstone of Communication:

- **What It Means to Listen Actively**: This isn't just about hearing what someone's saying. It's about tuning in, understanding their message, asking questions if you need to, and giving feedback that shows you get it. Active listening helps you collect all the info you need and grasp what the problem is.

Clear Communication: Getting the Point Across:

- **Keeping It Clear and Simple**: This is all about sharing information in a way easy to understand. Stick to plain language, steer clear of jargon, and maybe throw in some visuals if they'd help make things clearer.

Collaboration: Teaming Up for Better Solutions:

- **The Power of Working Together**: When you bring different people together to solve a problem, you get a mix of perspectives, skills, and knowledge. That can lead to some creative and out-of-the-box solutions. It's important to create an environment where everyone feels okay to speak up, where there's mutual respect, and where ideas can be freely exchanged.

Handling Communication Challenges:

- **Dealing with Bumps in the Road**: Communication isn't always smooth sailing. You might run into issues like people having different ways of communicating, personality clashes, language barriers, or trust issues in a team. The key to handling these challenges is to encourage open, respectful talk, promote active listening, and get everyone involved in team-building activities to strengthen those relationships.

In a nutshell, being able to communicate well and collaborate effectively is important in solving problems. Skills like active listening, clear communication, and encouraging teamwork can improve how you tackle problems. But remember, you might hit snags along the way. Tackling these head-on and making sure everyone's on the same page will keep your communication and collaboration on track.

~

OVERCOMING OBSTACLES AND STAYING PERSISTENT IN PROBLEM SOLVING

TACKLING obstacles and keeping your drive alive when solving problems can be tough. It's all about being resilient, flexible, and learning from the bumps along the way. Here are tips on how to get past these hurdles and stay on track:

Develop a Growth Mindset: Think of your skills as something you can build on. When you hit a snag, see it as a chance to grow, not just a barrier in your path. Keeping this positive outlook helps you stay motivated through tough times.

Break Down the Problem: Facing a huge problem can be daunting. Try breaking it into smaller bits. This makes it easier to handle, letting you focus on one thing at a time and gradually work your way through.

Seek Different Perspectives: If you're stuck, don't shy away from asking others for their thoughts. Fresh ideas and different views can shine a light on new solutions you might not have thought of. Plus, teaming up with others can give you a motivational boost.

Learn from Failures: Instead of getting down about things not working out, try to see each failure as a lesson. Think about what went wrong, figure out how to improve, and tweak your approach. Each misstep is a step closer to success.

Embrace Adaptability: Problem solving often means being ready to change your plan. Be open to new methods, different routes, and unexpected turns. This adaptability helps you get past unforeseen obstacles and discover creative solutions.

Take Breaks and Recharge: Working on a problem non-stop can wear you out. Step back now and then. A break can help clear your head and renew your energy.

Celebrate Small Wins: Every little success counts. Give yourself a pat on the back for the small achievements. These mini-celebrations can lift your spirits and keep you moving forward.

Manage Setbacks: When things don't go as planned, it's okay to feel bummed out, but don't linger on it. Look at setbacks as chances to learn and grow. They're just temporary hiccups on your way to reaching your goal.

Stay focused on the Goal: Keep your eyes on the prize. Remembering what you're working toward can help you push through the tough times. Picture the outcome you're aiming for and remind yourself why it's worth the effort.

Celebrate the Journey: It's not just about solving the problem – it's about what you learn and how you grow along the way. Enjoy the process, with all its ups and downs, as part of your journey in becoming a better problem solver.

By using these strategies, you can tackle obstacles and keep your persistence up when solving problems. Remember, being resilient, flexible, and learning from your missteps are key to finding those innovative solutions and succeeding. Stay motivated, focused, and enjoy the ride!

SECTION SIX WRAP-UP:

- **Why Problem-Solving Skills Matter:** Enhances decision-making, critical thinking, and confidence.

- **Systematic Approaches to Problem-Solving:** Use structured methods like the 5-Whys technique and fishbone diagrams.
- **Brainstorming for Creative Solutions:** Encourages collaborative and creative thinking.
- **Using a Decision Matrix:** Objectively evaluates solutions against criteria.
- **Feedback and Reflection:** Essential for improving problem-solving skills.
- **Define the Problem:** Clear understanding of the issue.
- **Gather Information:** Collect relevant data and insights.
- **Generate Alternative Solutions:** Creative brainstorming for multiple solutions.
- **Evaluate Options:** Assess pros and cons of each solution.
- **Implement the Chosen Solution:** Execute and track the solution.

- **Brainstorming Basics:** Generating a range of ideas.
- **Mind Mapping:** Visual approach to connect ideas.
- **Overcoming Creative Roadblocks:** Addressing barriers to creativity.
- **Diverse Perspectives:** Valuing different viewpoints.
- **Experimentation:** Trying and evolving ideas.
- **Objective Analysis:** Essential for fair problem-solving.
- **Pattern Recognition:** Identifying trends and correlations.
- **Evaluating Sources:** Critical for reliable information.
- **Reflective Thinking:** Personal introspection for better understanding.
- **Diverse Views and Logical Reasoning:** Broadening perspectives and making logical decisions.

ACTION ITEMS:

Practice the 5-Whys Technique: Regularly apply this method to dig into the root causes of problems.

Utilize Fishbone Diagrams: Use these for complex issues to visually break down potential causes.

Conduct Brainstorming Sessions: Regularly with team members or friends for diverse solutions.

Implement Decision Matrices: Use them to compare and focus on solutions for complex decisions.

Seek and Give Feedback: Regularly evaluate the effectiveness of your solutions and learn from outcomes.

- **Define Problems Clearly:** Write down problem statements for clarity.
- **Research Thoroughly:** Gather all necessary information before moving forward.
- **Brainstorm Solutions:** Alone or in a group, without judgment.
- **Evaluate Solutions:** Use criteria like feasibility and impact.

- **Plan and Execute Solutions:** Develop an action plan and follow through.
- **Regular Brainstorming:** Schedule sessions to encourage idea generation.
- **Create Mind Maps:** For project planning or problem-solving.
- **Challenge Assumptions:** Regularly question and explore new perspectives.
- **Encourage Teamwork:** Foster diverse team discussions.
- **Prototype and Test Ideas:** Implement and refine creative solutions.
- **Practice Objective Analysis:** Regularly assess situations without personal bias.
- **Identify Patterns:** Look for recurring themes in problems.
- **Critically Evaluate Sources:** Check the credibility of information.
- **Engage in Reflective Thinking:** Reflect on personal biases and thought processes.
- **Seek Various Perspectives:** Consult diverse groups for broader insights.

In Our Next Section:

In our next section, we'll dig into the transformative power of self-awareness and emotional intelligence in navigating life's complexities. Picture yourself as a skilled navigator, charting your course through the unpredictable seas of life. This part of our journey emphasizes understanding yourself deeply – your emotions, triggers, strengths, and areas for improvement. It's about turning the mirror inwards, gaining clarity on who you are, and how you react to the world around you. With this self-knowledge, you're not just reacting to life's events; you're responding with wisdom and insight.

Imagine harnessing the power of your emotions as a tool for growth, rather than obstacles to overcome. We'll explore strategies to enhance emotional intelligence – the ability to understand and manage your emotions and recognize and influence the emotions of others. This skill is essential for building stronger relationships, effective communication, and leadership. It's about becoming more empathetic, more in tune with others, and more capable of navigating social complexities. You'll learn how to transform emotional awareness into a strength that propels you toward personal and professional success, making you more resilient, adaptable, and fulfilled.

SECTION SEVEN: THE ROLE OF ADAPTABILITY IN NAVIGATING UNEXPECTED CHALLENGES

ADAPTABILITY: NAVIGATING LIFE'S SURPRISES

ADAPTABILITY, or the knack for rolling with the punches when things change, is important for both folks and organizations looking to handle life's curveballs well. In our fast-changing world, where you never know what's around the corner, being adaptable is more important than ever. It's like having a secret weapon that helps you respond well to unexpected stuff and get over hurdles.

What Adaptability Means:

- **Staying Open and Ready to Learn**: Being adaptable means you're open to new ideas and willing to learn and grow. It's about being flexible and able to switch up your game plan when needed. Instead of fighting change, adaptable people see it as a chance to develop and improve.

Why It's a Big Deal Now:

- **In a World Full of Surprises**: You never know when a new challenge might pop up, like an economic downturn, a natural disaster, a tech shake-up, or even personal hiccups. Being adaptable means you can think on your feet, make decisions fast, and act when needed.

The Perks of Being Adaptable:

- **Bouncing Back Stronger**: One of the coolest things about being adaptable is it helps you be resilient. When things don't go as planned, adaptable folks can quickly recover and find new ways to reach their goals. They don't get too bogged down by failure; instead, they learn from it and grow.

Adaptability in the Business World:

- **A Must for Companies, Too**: In the fast-moving business world, companies that can change and innovate are the ones that thrive. Companies that can't keep up with change often fall behind. Adaptability lets businesses spot new trends, respond to market changes, and try out new things, leading to better efficiency and success.

Feeling Confident Amidst Chaos:

- **Handling Uncertainty Like a Pro**: Being adaptable also means you can face uncertainty without freaking out. It gives you a sense of control even when things are wild. It's about facing challenges head-on, knowing you've got what it takes to adapt and overcome.

Wrapping Up: Adaptability is a key skill and mindset for dealing with unexpected challenges. It's all about embracing change, staying open to new ideas, and being resilient. This trait isn't just good for personal growth; it's a strategic edge in a world that's always changing. Whether you're an individual or a business, growing your adaptability skills means you're not just surviving the surprises life throws at you, but thriving through them.

THE PSYCHOLOGICAL SIDE OF ADAPTABILITY: RESILIENCE, FLEXIBILITY, AND OPENNESS

ADAPTABILITY IS like this mental superpower that helps us roll with life's punches and embrace change. It's made up of a few key parts: resilience, flexibility, and being open to new stuff. Let's dive into these parts to see how they help us deal with tough times, adapt to changes, and grab new opportunities.

Resilience: Bouncing Back Strong:

- **What It Is**: Resilience is like mental toughness. It's about getting back on your feet after life knocks you down. It's not about never feeling down but having the mental tools to recover and even come out stronger.
- **How It Works**: Resilient folks have a toolkit of psychological resources like staying optimistic, believing in themselves, being good at solving problems, and having a strong support network. It's not just about getting back to where you were, but growing and adapting to what life throws at you.

Flexibility: Adjusting on the Fly:

- **Being Adaptable in Thoughts and Actions**: Flexibility means you can change your thinking and how you act based on what's going on around you. It's about being open-minded, considering different points of view, and finding new ways to tackle problems. Flexible people see change as a chance to grow, not something to fear.
- **Stress Management**: If you're flexible, you're likely better at handling stress because you have more ways to cope.

Openness to New Experiences: Welcoming the New:

- **Eager to Explore and Learn**: This trait is all about being ready and willing to try new things, learn, and be open to fresh ideas and experiences. Open-minded people are curious about other cultures, keen to learn new stuff, and happy to challenge their own beliefs.
- **Fueling Creativity**: Being open to new experiences is often linked to creativity. It's about coming up with new ideas and solutions and being willing to step outside your comfort zone.

Wrapping It Up: Adaptability is a mix of being resilient, flexible, and open to new experiences. These traits shape how we handle tough times, adapt to changes, and seize new chances. And the great thing is, these aren't set in stone – you can work on developing them. So, by building up these qualities, you're not just getting through life's challenges; you're thriving and growing because of them.

REAL-LIFE TALES OF ADAPTABILITY: ENTREPRENEURS WHO TRIUMPHED AMIDST ECONOMIC CHALLENGES

Airbnb: In 2008, during the global recession, Airbnb founders Brian Chesky and Joe Gebbia faced a significant challenge. They were struggling to attract customers for their original idea of "AirBed & Breakfast", which involved renting out air mattresses in their living room for attendees of a design conference in San Francisco. However, they quickly adapted to the situation by creating a platform for short-term home rentals, which eventually became the successful business we know today.

Slack: Originally, Stewart Butterfield and his team developed a gaming platform called Glitch. Despite their efforts, Glitch did not gain traction. Instead of giving up, they pivoted and repurpose the internal communication tools they had built for their team during Glitch's development. This helped to create Slack, a wildly successful collaboration platform that is now used by millions of organizations globally.

Zoom: Eric Yuan, the CEO of Zoom, faced unexpected challenges during the 2008 economic downturn. He was working for a video conferencing company that had hit a roadblock due to the recession. Yuan adapted to the situation by leaving his job and founding Zoom in 2011. He believed there was a need for a simple and reliable video conferencing platform. Zoom quickly became popular and gained even more significance during the COVID-19 pandemic.

Nokia: Nokia was initially a paper mill company founded in 1865. Over the years, they diversified into various industries, including telecommunications. However, when new companies like Apple and Samsung revolutionized the mobile phone market, Nokia struggled to adapt to the smartphone era. Recognizing the need for change, Nokia sold its phone business to Microsoft and shifted focus toward industries like telecommunications infrastructure and networking, successfully navigating the unexpected challenge.

IBM: In the 1980s, IBM faced a significant challenge when they realized that their mainframe computers were becoming less popular due to the rise of personal computers. However, instead of being complacent, IBM adapted by developing the IBM Personal Computer (IBM PC). This decision let them capitalize on the growing demand for personal computers, enabling them to remain a major player in the technology industry.

These examples show how adaptability in the face of unexpected challenges can lead to successful outcomes. Entrepreneurs and companies that recognize and pivot in response to changing circumstances can often thrive and achieve long-term success.

THE UPSIDE OF BEING ADAPTABLE

ADAPTABILITY, or the knack for smoothly navigating through life's constant changes, is a useful skill. It's not just about handling what comes your way; it's about growing and thriving from these experiences. Let's talk about why being adaptable is such a game-changer.

Better Problem-Solving Skills:

- **Thinking On Your Feet**: Adaptable folks have a leg up when solving problems. They're cool with uncertainty and aren't thrown off by the unexpected. This means they're good at coming up with creative solutions and thinking outside the box, making them ace problem-solvers.

A More Positive Life Outlook:

- **Rolling with the Changes**: People who adapt easily usually see the glass as half full. They don't get stuck in negative thinking. Instead, they view change as a chance to grow and learn, which helps keep their spirits up, even when things get tough.

Building Resilience and Emotional Smarts:

- **Bouncing Back**: Being adaptable is like resilience training. It teaches you to get back up after life knocks you down. Plus, adapting often means seeing things from others' perspectives, which boosts your emotional smarts. This can help, whether you're working in a team or navigating daily life.

Personal Growth and Lifelong Learning:

- **Always Growing**: Adaptable folks are constantly learning. They're exposed to new experiences, ideas, and cultures, which broadens their view of the world. This curiosity and eagerness to learn mean they're always growing and evolving.

In Summary: Adaptability is more than just rolling with the punches. It's about becoming a better problem-solver, maintaining a positive attitude, building resilience and emotional intelligence, and being committed to personal growth and learning. Embracing adaptability means you're setting yourself up for success and contentment, no matter what life throws your way.

BOOSTING ADAPTABILITY: PRACTICAL STRATEGIES

ADAPTABILITY ISN'T JUST something you're born with. It's a skill you can grow. Here's how you can boost your adaptability and be ready for whatever comes your way:

Get Mindful: Mindfulness is all about living in the moment and accepting it without judgment. This practice sharpens your awareness of your thoughts and feelings, helping you understand yourself better. Being mindful helps you stay flexible and open, key traits for adaptability.

Dive into New Experiences: Want to build adaptability? Get out of your comfort zone. Whether it's traveling to unfamiliar places, picking up new hobbies, or taking on new roles at work, new experiences broaden your perspective and challenge you to adapt.

Embrace the Unknown: Uncertainty is a part of life. Learn to embrace it. Instead of resisting change, see it as a chance to grow. Letting go of the need for control can open up new possibilities and opportunities.

Sharpen Problem-Solving Skills: Improving your problem-solving abilities is a big part of becoming more adaptable. Tackle challenging situations that push your thinking. This could be anything from brain teasers to complex projects at work. Getting comfortable with tricky problems boosts your confidence in handling unexpected situations.

Surround Yourself with a Supportive Crew: Your adaptability can get a big boost from the people around you. Connect with folks who offer different viewpoints and are open to exploring new ideas. Conversations and collaborations with a diverse group can expand your thinking and provide a safety net for trying out new things.

Cultivate a Growth Mindset: Believe you can grow and improve, especially when faced with challenges. See setbacks as learning opportunities and failures as steps toward success. A positive attitude toward change and a commitment to learning new things are key for a growth mindset.

Take Care of Yourself: Your physical and mental well-being are important for adaptability. Regular exercise, a balanced diet, and enough sleep keep you energized. Practices like meditation or yoga can boost your mental resilience, making it easier to adapt in stressful times.

These strategies aren't just quick fixes; they're habits you can develop. By working on these areas, you can enhance your adaptability and navigate life's changes with more confidence and resilience.

THE POWER OF
ADAPTABILITY IN PERSONAL
GROWTH

ADAPTABILITY ISN'T JUST a handy skill; it's a game-changer in your journey of personal growth and self-improvement. Here's why being adaptable is so important:

Navigating Life's Twists and Turns: Life's full of surprises and not always the pleasant kind. Adaptability helps you deal with these curveballs. Instead of freezing up when things don't go as planned, being adaptable means you can switch gears, find new paths, and keep moving forward. It's about rolling with the punches and turning challenges into chances to grow.

Learning from the Tough Times: Everyone faces setbacks. The difference lies in how we handle them. If you're adaptable, you see these setbacks not as dead ends, but as detours with lessons along the way. Every time something doesn't work out, it's an opportunity to learn, tweak your approach, and come back stronger.

Stepping Out of the Comfort Zone: Real growth happens when you step out of what's familiar. Adaptability pushes you to do just that. It's about embracing new experiences, even when they feel scary or uncomfortable. When you're open to trying new things, you open doors to many opportunities and learning experiences.

Keeping a Positive Outlook: Let's face it, personal growth is not a straight path. It has its share of bumps and bruises. Being adaptable helps you keep a positive outlook through these ups and downs. It's about knowing that tough times are just temporary and seeing them as chances to grow and improve.

Adaptability is your superpower in the journey of personal growth. It helps you navigate life's unpredictable moments, learn from your mistakes, step outside your comfort zone, and keep a positive attitude through it all. By embracing adaptability, you're setting yourself up for continuous growth and transformation, getting ever closer to the best version of yourself.

ADAPTABILITY – YOUR KEY TO THRIVING IN A FAST-PACED WORLD

THE WORLD we live in is a whirlwind of change. Every day brings something new – sometimes exciting, sometimes challenging. In this ever-shifting landscape, adaptability isn't just nice to have; it's essential. It's the golden ticket to not just surviving, but actually thriving, amid all the twists and turns life throws our way.

Here's Why Adaptability Rocks:

- **Riding the Wave of Change**: Gone are the days when things were predictable and stable. Now, it's all about rapid technological shifts, economic roller coasters, and global uncertainties. To keep up, we've got to be ready to pivot, shift gears, and embrace new ways of doing things. Sticking to old habits? That's a surefire recipe for getting left far behind.
- **Seizing Opportunities**: The beauty of being adaptable is that it helps you spot and grab opportunities that others might miss. When you're flexible and open to change, you can ride the crest of innovation and use it to your advantage.
- **Bouncing Back**: Let's not sugarcoat it – setbacks are part of the game. But with adaptability in your toolkit, you can take those

setbacks in stride, learn from them, and come back even stronger.

- **The COVID-19 Lesson**: If there's one thing the pandemic has taught us, adaptability is important. The folks who quickly shifted to new ways of working, communicating, and living managed to keep their heads above water.

Embracing Adaptability for Growth: Adapting isn't always easy. It means letting go of the familiar and stepping into the unknown. It calls for a mindset shift, a willingness to constantly learn and relearn. But the payoff? Huge. By becoming adaptable, you open yourself up to a world of possibilities. You become resilient, ready to face any challenge with a 'bring it on' attitude.

So, here's the deal: let's lean into adaptability. Let's be those eager learners, innovators, and changemakers. Let's not shy away from the new and the uncertain. Instead, let's embrace it as a chance to grow and excel. By doing this, we're not just navigating through a world of constant change; we're shaping our own paths, carving out our own successes, and thriving like never.

SECTION SEVEN WRAP-UP:

ADAPTABILITY IN NAVIGATING Life's Surprises

- **Importance of Adaptability**: Essential for handling unexpected changes and challenges.
- **Resilience**: Key part of adaptability, enabling quick recovery from setbacks.
- **Flexibility**: Important for adjusting thoughts and actions to new situations.
- **Openness**: Welcoming new experiences and ideas enhances adaptability.

Psychological Aspects of Adaptability

- **Resilience**: Mental toughness to bounce back and grow from challenges.
- **Flexibility**: Adjusting thinking and behavior to suit changing circumstances.

- **Openness**: Eagerness to explore and learn from new experiences.

Real-Life Examples of Adaptability

- **Entrepreneurial Pivots**: Instances where adaptability led to business success.
- **Corporate Adaptations**: Examples of companies successfully navigating major industry shifts.

Upsides of Being Adaptable

- **Enhanced Problem-Solving**: Adaptable individuals excel in creative solutions.
- **Positive Life Outlook**: Change is seen as an opportunity for growth.
- **Emotional Intelligence**: Improved through diverse experiences.

ACTION ITEMS:

Boosting Adaptability

- **Practice Mindfulness**: To improve awareness and openness to change.
- **Seek New Experiences**: Step out of comfort zones to enhance adaptability.
- **Embrace Uncertainty**: Learn to be comfortable with not knowing.
- **Develop Problem-Solving Skills**: Tackle challenging situations to improve adaptability.
- **Nurture a Support Network**: Connect with diverse individuals for broader perspectives.
- **Cultivate a Growth Mindset**: View challenges as opportunities for learning.
- **Focus on Self-Care**: Maintain physical and mental well-being.

Building a Support Network

- **Identify Key Individuals**: Determine who can offer valuable support and guidance.
- **Strengthen Relationships**: Through open communication and mutual support.
- **Respect Boundaries**: Understand and respect limits within your support network.
- **Show Appreciation**: Express gratitude and reciprocate support.

Adapting for Personal Growth

- **Navigate Life's Challenges**: Use adaptability to manage life's unpredictability.
- **Learn from Difficulties**: View setbacks as learning opportunities.
- **Venture Beyond Comfort**: Embrace new experiences for personal development.
- **Maintain a Positive Attitude**: Stay optimistic through changing circumstances.

Thriving in a Fast-Paced World

- **Embrace Change**: Adapt to technological and societal shifts.
- **Recognize Opportunities**: Use adaptability to seize new chances.
- **Learn from the Pandemic**: Apply lessons from COVID-19 to future challenges.
- **Develop Continuous Learning**: Commit to lifelong learning and adaptation.

By focusing on these key points and putting the action into practice items, you can enhance your adaptability, making it easier to navigate life's constant changes and challenges effectively.

• • •

In Our Next Section:

In our next section, we're diving into the art of effective decision-making – a critical skill for navigating life's twists and turns with confidence and clarity. Decision-making is more than just choosing between options; it's about understanding the impact of your choices, balancing risk and reward, and steering your journey toward your goals. We'll explore how to cut through the noise, weigh your options, and make decisions that align with your goals and values.

Imagine facing a crossroads with the tools to evaluate each path and the wisdom to choose the one that leads you toward success and fulfillment. That's the power of effective decision-making. We'll give you practical strategies to enhance your decision-making process, whether in personal life or professional settings. Get ready to transform the way you make choices – turning decision-making from a daunting task into an empowering skill that propels you forward on your path to success.

SECTION EIGHT: IDENTIFYING AND UTILIZING AVAILABLE RESOURCES

NAVIGATING THROUGH YOUR RESOURCES FOR SUCCESS

ALL RIGHT LET'S talk about making the most of what you've got. Whether you're flying solo or running a team, knowing your resources and how to use them is key to hitting those targets. This chapter is all about figuring out what you have in your arsenal and how to make it work for you.

1. What Counts as Resources? First things first, let's define 'resources.' We're talking about anything you can use to get stuff done. This could be stuff you can touch, like cash or computers (tangible resources), or things you can't, like your know-how, network, or the good rep you've built (intangible resources).

2. Spotting Your Resources: Now, how do you figure out what you've got? It's about looking around and within. It's not just about spotting the obvious stuff but also uncovering hidden gems you might not have thought to use before.

2.1. The Tangible Stuff: Here, we're diving into the things you can physically count or touch. Money in the bank, the tech you use, the physical space you've got – all these count. It's also worth checking out their current condition and how you can jazz them up to serve you better.

2.2. The Intangible Gold: These are your unseen assets. Your personal knowledge, the unique skills you or your team have, the relationships you've built, and even your reputation in the field. Understanding these requires a deeper dig into what you or your organization can uniquely offer.

3. Measuring What You've Got: Once you've listed out your resources, it's time to weigh them up. How far can these resources take you? Are they enough for what you want to achieve? How do they stack up in terms of quality and effectiveness?

3.1. Assessing Scope: Here's where you figure out how wide-ranging your resources are. Can they adapt to different situations? Are there ways to stretch them further or use them in new ways?

3.2. Understanding Strengths: Now, let's talk about power. How strong are your resources? Are they something unique that sets you apart? How easily can they be copied or replaced? Knowing this helps you figure out where to focus your efforts.

4. Getting the Full Picture: To get a handle on your resources, you might need to mix things up a bit. Think surveys, chats with your team, diving into data, or even seeing how you stack up against competitors. A mix of approaches can give you a clearer view.

Conclusion: Getting a grip on your resources – what they are, how strong they are, and how far they can go – is a massive step toward meeting your goals. It's about making informed choices, playing to your strengths, and getting creative with what you have. So, look closely around and within, and get ready to make the most of your resources. Let's turn those assets into achievements!

NAVIGATING EXTERNAL RESOURCES: YOUR ROADMAP TO SUCCESS

To effectively achieve your goals and address your specific needs, it is important to be aware of the external resources that are available to you. These resources can range from government programs and grants to community organizations and educational institutions. This chapter aims to give you practical tips on how to identify and assess these resources, enabling you to make informed decisions and maximize your chances of success.

1. Government Programs: Let's talk government programs first. These guys can offer you everything from cash to connections. Your starting point? Hit up the websites of local, state, and national governments. Keep your eyes peeled for programs that fit your field or particular needs. Important stuff to check: who can apply, when you gotta apply by, and how much dough they're dishing out.

Once you've got a few programs on your radar, dig deeper. What's the program's main goal? What kind of help are they offering? Got questions? Contact the folks running the show. They're usually happy to help you out.

2. Grants: Grants are like the golden ticket of resources – free money, but with a purpose. You can find these gems through foundations, non-profits, research bodies, and professional groups. Look for ones that resonate with your goals.

Now, assessing grants is a bit like detective work. What do they need from you? What's the cash limit? And how do they decide who wins? Keep an eye out for any strings attached, like how you have to report your progress.

3. Community Organizations: Community organizations are your go-to for support and networking. You can find these at various levels – local, regional, national. A good way to start is by asking around – your workmates, mentors, or others in your field. Or just Google it.

When checking out these orgs, think about what you need. How much does it cost to join? How much time should you commit? What can they offer you? Sometimes, the best way to figure this out is to just dive in – go to an event or two and chat with members.

4. Educational Institutions: Universities and colleges aren't just for studying; they're gold mines for resources like research, training, and team-ups. Consider their websites, especially for programs or departments that line up with your interests. Workshops, seminars, partnerships – it's all up for grabs.

To see if an institution is right for you, check out what resources and knowledge they have, their standing in the field, and what collaborations they've done before. Don't shy away from contacting faculty or program heads for more info.

Chapter Conclusion: Wrapping up, getting the right external resources is a big part of hitting your targets. Whether it's government programs, grants, community orgs, or educational institutions, there's a lot out there. Remember to do your homework – understand what these resources offer, how they align with your goals, and what you need to do to snag them. With the right approach, these resources can be a game-changer in your journey to success.

HARNESSING WHAT'S ALREADY THERE: UNLOCKING INTERNAL RESOURCES

Recognizing and using internal resources is important for individuals and organizations to maximize their potential and succeed. This chapter will discuss the significance of self-awareness, skills assessment, and collaboration within teams to tap into existing knowledge, expertise, and talent.

1. Self-Awareness: Know Thyself First up, we've got self-awareness. This is about knowing your own strengths and where you need a boost. It's like taking an honest look in the mirror and figuring out what you're good at and where you could do better. When you get this, you can use your strong points to the max and work on the areas that need some TLC. This isn't just good for you; it's great for your team or company too. When you know your superpowers, you can use them to help everyone smash their goals.

2. Skills Assessment: Taking Stock Next, we need to chat about sizing up the skills you've got on your team. It's like inventorying all the awesome talents everyone brings to the table. This step is helpful because it lets you see what you're working with. Where are the gaps? What strengths do you have in spades? This knowledge is golden because it helps to figure out who should do what and where you might need to bring in new blood or level up some skills.

3. Team Collaboration: Stronger Together And then, there's team-work. When folks collaborate, magic happens. It's all about pooling everyone's skills, experiences, and ideas. When you create a space where everyone feels comfy sharing and bouncing ideas around, you're basically setting the stage for some top-notch problem-solving and innovation. Collaboration builds trust and means everyone's playing to their strengths while supporting each other in the not-so-strong areas. Result? The whole team wins!

Wrap-Up: Putting It All Together So, there you have it. Tapping into internal resources is key for both individuals and organizations wanting to reach their peak. Being self-aware, knowing what skills you've got, and rocking collaboration can turn a good team into an unstoppable force. It's all about using what you already have to its fullest potential. Get these things right, and you're well on your way to nailing those goals.

$\sim$

BUILDING NETWORKS AND SEEKING PARTNERSHIPS:

IN TODAY'S INTERCONNECTED WORLD, no organization can thrive in isolation. The ability to tap into available resources and form strategic partnerships has become essential for succeeding. This chapter explores the role of networking and partnerships in identifying and leveraging resources, providing strategies and tips on establishing relationships, engaging with stakeholders, and harnessing collaborations to maximize the benefits of shared resources.

1.1 Networking: Your Key to Unveiling Hidden Resources

- **Discovering Resources through Connections:** Networking is like having a treasure map in the professional world. It connects you with people and organizations, opening doors to a wealth of information, collaboration, and resources that might otherwise stay hidden.
- **Networking in Action:** for example, a businessperson brainstorming a new product can gain invaluable insights by mingling with marketing gurus or design wizards at networking events or online. These connections can lead to specialized knowledge or even unexpected partnerships.

1.2 Linking Up with Potential Partners and Stakeholders

- **Using Networking as a Radar:** Think of networking as your radar for spotting potential allies and supporters for your projects. It's about building bridges with people and organizations that share your vision and goals.
- **Strategies for Building Networks:** Hit up industry gatherings or join online professional groups to cast your net wider. Don't forget to use your existing contacts – sometimes, the right connection is a conversation away.

1.3 Networking for Expert Insights and Wisdom

- **Connecting with the Pros:** Networking is your ticket to the inner circle of industry experts and thought leaders. These are the folks who've been there, done that, and have valuable nuggets of wisdom to share.
- **Ways to Build Relationships with Experts:** Jump into industry events, interact with experts on social media, or find a mentor. Offer value in these interactions – it's not just about what you can get, but also what you can contribute.

Utilizing Professional Networks for Knowledge Exchange

- **Sharing Brainspace:** Professional networks are like a giant, collective brain. They're perfect for swapping ideas, getting fresh perspectives, and even teaming up for projects.
- **Tips for Active Networking:** Engage in professional groups, share your know-how, and don't be shy to ask for advice. Remember, a strong network thrives on give and take – it's about building a community, not just a contact list.

PART 2: LAYING THE FOUNDATIONS OF STRONG RELATIONSHIPS

2.1 BUILDING TRUST: SOLIDIFYING SUCCESSFUL PARTNERSHIPS

- **Communicate Openly and Honestly:** Transparency is the bedrock of trust. This involves genuinely sharing information, tackling misunderstandings swiftly, and respecting each other's viewpoints.
- **Align Words and Actions:** Trust grows when what we say matches what we do. Being reliable, meeting deadlines, and keeping promises cultivates predictability and confidence in a partnership.
- **Acknowledge and Own Up:** Accepting responsibility for your actions, especially when things go awry, shows integrity and dedication to the partnership.
- **Empathy and Respect:** Show understanding and consideration for your partner's perspectives, especially during disagreements. This fosters an environment of collaborative problem-solving.

2.2 Engaging with Stakeholders: Nurturing Beneficial Connections

- **Identifying Stakeholders:** Understand who is crucial to your project or organization. This could range from employees and shareholders to customers, suppliers, and community members.
- **Understand Their Needs:** Once identified, dive into understanding their expectations and concerns. This might involve interviews, surveys, or direct discussions to gather their views.

- **Effective Communication:** Tailor your communication plan to suit each stakeholder group. Keep them informed and involved.
- **Building Relationships:** Trust and openness are key. Listen to their feedback, acknowledge their concerns, and work on creating mutual understanding and respect.
- **Addressing Their Needs:** Use the insights gathered to meet their expectations effectively. This might mean adjusting project plans or policies.
- **Regular Reevaluation:** Stakeholder priorities can shift, so regularly reassess your approach to ensure it aligns with their evolving needs.
- **Supportive Networks:** Building a network means more than collecting contacts. It's about forming genuine connections, offering and receiving support, and sharing resources.
- **Professional Networks for Knowledge Exchange:** By participating in professional networks, you tap into a collective knowledge pool, stay updated with industry trends, and gain access to new resources.

Part Two Conclusion:

• **Networking and Relationship Building:** Whether it's with stakeholders, within a professional network, or in a partnership, building trust, engaging effectively, and exchanging knowledge are important. These connections are not just about expanding your contact list but about creating a community where everyone grows together.

PART THREE: HARNESSING THE POWER OF COLLABORATION

3.1 Partnering with Complementary Organizations: Finding the Right Collaborative Fit

- **Understand Your Own Goals First:** Before you can find the right partners, be crystal clear about what your organization aims to achieve. What are your core values, mission, and the areas where collaboration could be most fruitful?

- **Research Potential Partners:** Look within and beyond your industry. Use online tools, go to events, and leverage your network to find organizations that complement your mission and goals.
- **Networking Events:** These are goldmines for finding potential collaborators. Engage in discussions, participate in activities, and keep an open mind to all possibilities.
- **Use Your Existing Network:** Sometimes, the best connections come from those you already know. Spread the word about your search for partners and see who surfaces from your own network.
- **Industry Associations and Online Platforms:** These are great places to find potential partners. They often host events and discussions where like-minded organizations converge.
- **Initiate Conversations:** Once you spot a potential partner, don't hesitate to reach out. Discuss how a partnership could be mutually beneficial and align with shared goals.

3.2 Synergizing Resources for Maximum Impact: Collaborative Efficiency

- **Technology Synergies:** In areas like tech, sharing resources like server space or software can slash costs and boost efficiency.
- **Broader Audience Reach:** By tapping into each other's networks, partnerships can extend their reach, benefiting from each other's audience and customer base.
- **Fostering Innovation:** Different perspectives coming together can spark creativity and lead to breakthroughs that wouldn't happen in isolation.
- **Knowledge Sharing:** Collaborations enable the exchange of insights and best practices, keeping all parties at the cutting edge of their fields.
- **Adapting and Adjusting:** Learn from each collaboration. Adapt your approaches based on what works best in a joint venture setting.

- **Cultivate Flexibility:** Be open to changing course as you learn from your collaborative experiences. Flexibility can lead to more successful outcomes.

3.3 Sharing Resources for Mutual Benefit: Collaborative Cost-Cutting

- **Tech and Facilities Sharing:** From software licenses to coworking spaces, sharing physical and tech resources can significantly cut costs.
- **Transportation Innovations:** Carpooling or ride-sharing can save money and reduce environmental footprints.
- **Knowledge Platforms:** Use online communities and collaborative tools to share knowledge and work together efficiently.
- **Collaborative R&D:** Share the risks and costs of innovation, leveraging each other's strengths for better, faster outcomes.
- **Fostering Sustainable Practices:** By sharing resources, organizations can adopt more sustainable practices, optimizing resource utilization.
- **Continuous Learning:** Stay open to learning from each collaboration. Every partnership offers new insights and ways to improve.

Part 3 Conclusion: Collaboration in networking isn't just about expanding your contacts; it's about creating meaningful partnerships that benefit everyone involved. Through thoughtful partnership selection, resource sharing, and embracing collaboration, organizations can amplify their impact, extend their reach, and unlock new opportunities for growth. Remember, the best collaborations are those where every party feels they're getting as much as they're giving.

PART 4: SMART NETWORKING STRATEGIES

4.1 Crafting a Winning Networking Strategy: Setting Goals and Targets

- **Clarify Your Goals:** Start with a clear understanding of what you want to achieve through networking. Is it more clients, a new job, or industry knowledge? Set specific, measurable goals.
- **Know Your Audience:** Figure out who you need to connect with to reach your goals. Who are the key players in your industry? What are the best groups to join?
- **Set Measurable Targets:** Make your networking goals real. Aim to go to a certain number of events each month or connect with a set number of people each week.
- **Focus Your Efforts:** Direct your networking toward activities that will most likely help you reach your goals. Choose the right events and groups for maximum impact.
- **Plan Your Time:** Lay out a timeline for your networking activities. Set deadlines and mini-goals to keep yourself on track.
- **Be Flexible:** Stay open to adjusting your plan. New opportunities might pop up that weren't on your radar before.
- **Track and Adjust:** Regularly review your progress. Are you meeting your networking targets? Adjust your strategy as needed.

4.2 A Systematic Approach to Networking: Building Your Network Step by Step

- **Define Clear Goals:** Understand exactly what you're networking for. Is it career advancement, learning opportunities, or industry insights?
- **Spot the Right Contacts:** Identify who can help you meet your networking goals. This might be industry leaders, peers with shared interests, or potential mentors.
- **Diverse Networking Channels:** Don't just stick to in-person events. Tap into online platforms, professional groups, and more to widen your networking scope.

- **Schedule Interactions:** Plan regular touchpoints with your network. This could be through social media, emails, or coffee meetings.
- **Be Genuine and Helpful:** Always approach your contacts with authenticity. Offer your help and knowledge wherever possible.
- **Listen and Learn:** Be an active listener in your interactions. You can learn a lot from what others have to say.
- **Keep Organized and Track Progress:** Use tools to keep your contacts and interactions organized. Regularly check how close you are to your networking goals.
- **Evaluate and Tweak Your Approach:** Constantly assess how effective your networking is. Change your strategy where necessary.

4.3 Making the Most of Online Networking: Mastering Digital Connections

- **Choose the Right Platforms:** Select online platforms that align with your professional goals. LinkedIn, Twitter, or industry-specific forums can be great starting points.
- **Optimize Your Profile:** Your online profile is your first impression. Make it count with a professional photo and a bio that highlights your skills and goals.
- **Join Relevant Groups:** Engage with online groups that align with your interests. Participate in discussions to showcase your expertise.
- **Share and Contribute Value:** Regularly post insightful content and engage with others' posts. It's a great way to show your knowledge and stay visible.
- **Connect and Engage Authentically:** Reach out to professionals with personalized messages. Show genuine interest in their work.
- **Virtual Events and Webinars:** Attend online events to learn and network. Be active in discussions and follow up with new connections afterwards.

- **Give and Take:** Networking is reciprocal. Offer assistance to your contacts whenever you can.
- **Stay Connected:** Regularly engage with your network to keep relationships alive. Comment on updates, share interesting articles, and check in sometimes.

4.4 Engaging in Online Communities: Maximizing Your Digital Presence

- **Identify Key Communities:** Find online forums and communities relevant to your industry or interests. Look for active groups where real discussions take place.
- **Observe Before Diving In:** Take time to understand the community's dynamics. What's the etiquette? What kinds of discussions happen?
- **Share Your Expertise:** Contribute to discussions with valuable insights and advice. It's a great way to prove yourself to be a knowledgeable professional.
- **Engage with Peers:** Don't just post and vanish. Respond to comments, join conversations, and show genuine interest in others' opinions.
- **Show Gratitude and Reciprocate:** Always thank others for their insights and offer help in return. Networking is a two-way street.
- **Professional Online Behavior:** Maintain professionalism in all your online interactions. Respectful and constructive communication is key.
- **Expand Relationships Beyond Platforms:** Take promising online connections to the next level. Connect on LinkedIn, or propose a virtual coffee chat.
- **Constant Learning and Adapting:** Keep learning from each interaction and refine your approach based on what works best in these online communities.

By implementing these strategies, you can create an effective and dynamic networking approach that helps you meet your professional goals while building meaningful connections. Remember, networking is a skill that improves with practice, so stay engaged, be genuine, and keep refining your approach for the best results.

NAILING RESOURCE MANAGEMENT: MAKING THE MOST OF WHAT YOU HAVE

EFFECTIVE RESOURCE MANAGEMENT techniques are important in today's fast-paced and competitive business environment. Organizations need to optimize their resources to ensure maximum efficiency and productivity. This chapter will dig into the importance of developing these techniques and explore various ideas that can help achieve this optimization.

1. Prioritizing: What's Top of the List? First things first: prioritizing. Think of it like sorting your to-do list by what's urgent and important. This is all about figuring out which tasks should get your attention first. It's like putting the big rocks in the jar before the small stones. When you nail this, you make sure you're spending time and energy on the stuff that moves the needle, and not just busywork.

2. Delegating: Sharing the Load Then, there's delegating. This is about playing matchmaker between tasks and the people best equipped to handle them. It's like being a coach, knowing which player to put in for each play. Delegating not only shares the workload but also taps into the unique skills and strengths your team offers. It's about trusting your team to do their thing and do it well.

3. Budgeting: Keeping an Eye on the Dollars Budgeting is a biggie. Here, you're playing a balancing act with your finances. It's about planning out where your bucks will get the most bang for your buck. Budgeting means you're less likely to find yourself in a pickle financially because you've got a clear plan for your resources. It's like planning your road trip with enough gas in the tank.

4. Time Management: Every Minute Counts And let's not forget about time management. This is all about making every second count. It's planning your day, week, or project timeline in a way that you're not just busy – you're productive. Good time management stops tasks from dragging on and helps you hit those deadlines without a last-minute scramble.

The Big Picture: Why This Matters So why bother with all this? Well, effective resource management means you're squeezing every bit of value out of your resources. You're not just throwing money, time, or people at problems – you're using them smartly. This leads to better productivity, smarter spending, and a smoother ride in handling the ups and downs of business.

In a Nutshell To wrap it up, getting your resource management on point is like having a roadmap for success. It's about knowing what to do, who should do it, how much you can spend on it, and how long it should take. Nail these, and you're well on your way to making your organization not just run, but sprint toward its goals.

TACKLING RESOURCE LIMITATIONS: SMART STRATEGIES FOR SUCCESS

TODAY, it is becoming increasingly clear that resources are not infinite. Whether it is the scarcity of natural resources or the limited availability of time, constraints on resources can pose significant challenges in various domains of life. This chapter aims to address these challenges and provide strategies for adapting and finding alternatives when faced with resource limitations.

1. Embrace Creativity: When you're up against resource limitations, it's all about getting creative. Think of it like a puzzle where you've got to make the most of what you've got. It's about repurposing what you have, challenging the usual way of doing things, and seeing possibilities instead of roadblocks. It's time to put on your thinking cap and get innovative!

2. Hone Problem-Solving Skills: Problem-solving is your best friend when resources are tight. You've got to dig into the root of issues and come up with solid solutions. Maybe it's brainstorming with your team, getting advice from pros, or breaking down big challenges into smaller bits. It's like being a detective, piecing together clues to make the most of what you have.

3. Cultivate Resilience: Now, resilience is key. Facing resource limitations isn't always a smooth ride. There will be hiccups, maybe even failures. But, it's about getting back up, dusting yourself off, and keeping on. It's that never-say-die attitude and learning from setbacks that keep you moving forward.

4. Master Resource Management: Resource management is a game-changer. Let's talk about focusing on – it's like choosing which balls to juggle when you've got too many in the air. Focus on what's most important first. Then there's delegation – it's handing out tasks to the right people, making sure everyone's playing to their strengths.

5. Budget Wisely: When it comes to money, it's all about smart budgeting. It's planning your spending, keeping an eye on costs, and looking for affordable options. Think of it as making every dollar count.

6. Time Management: And let's not forget time – it's as precious as money. Time management means lining up your ducks in a row, setting doable deadlines, and cutting out the fluff. It's about making every second count.

The Bottom Line: Briefly, when you're facing resource limitations, it's about being smart, resourceful, and resilient. Whether it's squeezing the most out of every penny, making the best use of time, or thinking outside the box, these strategies will help you navigate through tight spots. Remember, it's not about the size of the resource pool; it's about how you use it. Dive in, and make waves with what you've got!

~

SECTION EIGHT WRAP-UP:

KEY POINTS:

NAVIGATING Through Your Resources for Success

- **What Counts as Resources**: Includes tangible (money, tech, space) and intangible resources (knowledge, skills, network).
- **Spotting Your Resources**: Assess both physical and abstract assets, looking for obvious and hidden resources.
- **Measuring What You've Got**: Evaluate the extent, scope, and strength of your resources.
- **Getting the Full Picture**: Use various methods like surveys and data analysis to understand your resources.

Navigating External Resources: Your Roadmap to Success

- **Government Programs**: Seek relevant government programs and understand their criteria.
- **Grants**: Identify and assess grants suitable for your goals.
- **Community Organizations**: Utilize local and national organizations for support and networking.

- **Educational Institutions**: Leverage resources from educational institutions for research and training.

Harnessing What's Already There: Unlocking Internal Resources

- **Self-Awareness**: Understand your strengths and areas for improvement.
- **Skills Assessment**: Identify and evaluate the skills within your team or organization.
- **Team Collaboration**: Utilize collaborative efforts to pool skills and ideas.

Building Networks and Seeking Partnerships:

- **Networking**: Utilize networking for discovering resources and forming alliances.
- **Trust Building**: Focus on building trust in partnerships through open communication.
- **Engaging Stakeholders**: Effectively engage with stakeholders to understand and address their needs.
- **Collaboration**: Seek partnerships with complementary organizations for resource sharing and innovation.

Nailing Resource Management: Making the Most of What You Have

- **Focusing on**: Focus on urgent and important tasks.
- **Delegating**: Assign tasks based on team members' strengths.
- **Budgeting**: Plan and manage finances wisely.
- **Time Management**: Utilize effective time management strategies.

Tackling Resource Limitations: Smart Strategies for Success

- **Embrace Creativity**: Find innovative solutions within resource constraints.

- **Problem-Solving Skills**: Enhance problem-solving abilities to tackle challenges.
- **Resilience**: Develop resilience to recover from setbacks.
- **Resource Management**: Prioritize and delegate effectively under limitations.

Case studies and real-life examples:

- **Business Growth**: Small business leveraging unused assets for growth.
- **Nonprofit Impact**: Nonprofit organization using collaborations to address homelessness.
- **Individual Contribution**: An individual using personal resources for community improvement.

ACTION ITEMS:

Navigating Through Your Resources for Success

- **Inventory Resources**: List all physical and abstract resources available to you.
- **Resource Evaluation**: Assess the condition and potential of each resource.
- **Resource Diversification**: Explore ways to expand or improve existing resources.

Navigating External Resources: Your Roadmap to Success

- **Research Programs**: Search and apply for relevant government programs and grants.
- **Join Organizations**: Become active in community organizations and professional groups.
- **Connect with Institutions**: Engage with educational institutions for partnerships and resources.

Harnessing What's Already There: Unlocking Internal Resources

- **Self-Assessment**: Conduct a personal skills and strengths assessment.
- **Team Skill Mapping**: Map out the skills and talents within your team.
- **Encourage Collaboration**: Foster a culture of collaboration and idea-sharing.

Building Networks and Seeking Partnerships:

- **Network Expansion**: Go to industry events and participate in online professional groups.
- **Build Trust**: Cultivate trust through consistent and open communication.
- **Stakeholder Engagement**: Regularly communicate with stakeholders to align goals and expectations.
- **Seek Partnerships**: Identify and approach potential partner organizations for collaborations.

Nailing Resource Management: Making the Most of What You Have

- **Prioritize Tasks**: Use tools like the Eisenhower Matrix for task prioritization.
- **Delegate Effectively**: Match tasks with team members' strengths and skills.
- **Budget Planning**: Create and maintain a detailed budget plan.
- **Manage Time**: Implement time management techniques like the Pomodoro Technique.

Tackling Resource Limitations: Smart Strategies for Success

- **Innovate Solutions**: Brainstorm creative solutions for resource limitations.
- **Improve Problem-Solving**: Practice regular problem-solving exercises.
- **Build Resilience**: Develop resilience through mindfulness and stress management techniques.

- **Master Resource Management**: Regularly review and adjust resource management strategies.

Case Studies and Real-Life Examples:

- **Study Cases**: Analyze provided case studies for insights and lessons.
- **Apply Learnings**: Implement strategies and solutions from the case studies in your context.
- **Share Insights**: Discuss case studies with peers or team members for broader perspectives.

In Our Next Section:

In our next section, we'll dig into the transformative power of positive relationships and community support. It's a fact that we're social beings, and our connections with others can have a huge impact on our lives. We'll explore how building and nurturing positive relationships can elevate our personal and professional lives. From cultivating deep connections with family and friends to forging collaborative and supportive professional networks, we'll uncover the benefits of surrounding ourselves with people who uplift and inspire us.

We'll discuss the role of community involvement in enhancing our sense of purpose and belonging. Engaging with your community, whether through volunteer work, local initiatives, or group activities, not only contributes to societal well-being but also enriches your own life. By participating in collective efforts and contributing to the greater good, you open doors to new experiences, perspectives, and a profound sense of fulfillment. Get ready to learn how to harness the strength of your relationships and community ties to build a more connected, fulfilling, and impactful life.

SECTION NINE: PRACTICING SELF-COMPASSION AND SELF-CARE DURING CHALLENGING TIMES

NAVIGATING TOUGH TIMES: THE KEY ROLE OF SELF-COMPASSION AND SELF-CARE

SELF-COMPASSION: **Your Inner Ally**

- **Understanding Self-Compassion:** It's about being a friend to yourself, especially when the going gets tough. Imagine giving yourself the same kindness and understanding you'd offer a good friend. It's recognizing your struggles and meeting them with empathy and warmth.
- **Why It Matters:** Self-compassion is like a safety net for your emotions. It helps you deal with tough feelings, cuts down on self-criticism, and brings a sense of calm and inner strength. It's a way of reminding yourself that it's okay to be human and make mistakes.
- **Changing the Inner Dialogue:** Often, we're our own worst critics. We beat ourselves up over things beyond our control or decisions that didn't pan out. Self-compassion shifts this narrative. It's about replacing harsh self-talk with a more understanding and supportive voice.

Self-Care: Recharging Your Batteries

- **The Essence of Self-Care:** Think of self-care as maintenance for your overall well-being. About doing things replenish your energy, ease stress, and keep you feeling balanced. It's not just a luxury; it's a necessity.
- **Busting Self-Care Myths:** There's this idea that looking after yourself is selfish or a luxury for when you've ticked off everything else. But that's not the case. Neglecting self-care can leave you drained and less able to handle life's pressures.
- **What Self-Care Looks Like:** It's different for everyone. Maybe it's going for a run, meditating, writing in your journal, or chilling in the park. The aim is to find what gives you a sense of peace and joy and make time for it, regularly.

Why It's Essential

- **Like Putting on Your Oxygen Mask:** Ever heard that airplane safety spiel about oxygen masks? The same logic applies here. You've got to take care of yourself first to be there effectively for others.
- **Beyond Personal Benefits:** Practicing self-compassion and self-care doesn't just help you; it helps you be your best for the people around you. It boosts your emotional resilience, your ability to be compassionate to others, and helps you handle life's curveballs with more grace.
- **Self-Care in Action:** It's all about commitment. Identify what lifts you up and incorporate it into your routine. Whether it's quiet time in the morning, a hobby you love, or regular check-ins with friends, make it a non-negotiable part of your life.

Wrapping It Up To sum it up, self-compassion and self-care are your allies in navigating life's tough patches. They're about treating yourself with kindness and ensuring you're well-equipped to face life's challenges. By embracing these practices, you're not just surviving; you're setting yourself up to thrive, even in the face of adversity.

~

UNDERSTANDING YOUR EMOTIONS AND CHALLENGES

RECOGNIZING and acknowledging one's emotions and challenges is a crucial part of emotional intelligence and self-awareness. It involves being honest with oneself and taking the time to reflect on and understand our own feelings and difficulties.

Getting to Know Your Emotions:

- **Spotting Your Feelings:** It's about tuning into your emotions, noticing how you feel in different situations. Keep an eye out for those physical clues and thoughts that pop up when emotions are in play. Remember, there's no wrong way to feel – every emotion is part of the human experience.
- **Embracing Your Emotions:** Once you've figured out what you're feeling, the next step is to accept these emotions. This means not shying away from or pushing down your feelings, even the tough ones. Give yourself the space to feel and experience them.

Facing Your Challenges Head-On:

- **Recognizing the Rough Patches:** This part's about seeing and accepting the tough spots in your life. It could be anything – personal struggles, work issues, areas where you know you can do better. It's about being real with yourself about where you're at and what you're facing.
- **Learning from Challenges:** When you see your challenges, it opens the door to self-kindness and understanding. It's a chance to reflect, grow, and build that inner strength. Ask yourself, "How can I get past this?" or "What can I learn from this?"
- **Talking About It:** Recognizing your emotions and challenges isn't just a solo journey. It also helps you communicate better with others. Being open about your feelings and what you're going through can strengthen your relationships and make it easier to get support.

Wrapping Up: To sum it up, understanding your emotions and challenges is key to personal growth and emotional smarts. It's about being in tune with your feelings, accepting them, and facing your challenges with honesty. This way, you're not only getting to know yourself better but also laying the groundwork for healthier, more open connections with others.

GROWING SELF-COMPASSION: EMBRACING NON-JUDGMENT AND KINDNESS TO YOURSELF

SELF-COMPASSION IS like being your own best friend. It's about being kind, understanding, and accepting toward yourself, just as you would be to someone you care about. The keys to nurturing this self-compassion are learning to let go of self-judgment and practicing self-kindness. Let's break down how these can make a big difference in how we treat ourselves:

Letting Go of Self-Judgment:

- **Catch Those Critical Thoughts:** We've all got that inner critic, constantly nitpicking at our actions, looks, or skills. These harsh judgments can knock down our self-esteem.
- **Be Your Own Cheerleader:** When you find yourself being self-critical, pause and remind yourself that it's okay to be imperfect. Remember, no one's flawless, and expecting ourselves to be is setting the bar unrealistically high.
- **Create a Supportive Inner Voice:** Instead of feeding into those self-critical thoughts, try shifting to a more supportive inner dialogue. It's about giving yourself the same grace and understanding you'd offer a good friend.

Embracing Self-Kindness:

- **Treat Yourself Like a Friend:** We're often kinder to others than we are to ourselves. It's time to extend that same kindness inward. How would you comfort a friend? Try offering that same comfort to yourself.
- **Nurture Yourself:** Indulge in things that make you feel cared for. Whether it's taking a relaxing bath, reading a good book, or simply allowing yourself some downtime, it's about showing yourself some love.
- **Positive Self-Talk:** Use words of encouragement and support when talking to yourself. It's like being your own personal cheerleader.

Blending non-judgment with self-kindness helps foster self-compassion. It's a journey, for sure. Shifting from a critical to a caring mindset takes time and practice. But stick with it, and you'll gradually see a change in how you relate to yourself.

Growing self-compassion through non-judgment and self-kindness is about embracing your imperfections, acknowledging your humanity, and wrapping yourself in warmth and understanding. As you cultivate this self-compassion, you'll find you're better equipped to face life's ups and downs with a stronger, kinder heart.

NAVIGATING THE SELF-CARE JOURNEY: DISCOVERING WHAT FITS YOU BEST

Self-care isn't one-size-fits-all. It's about figuring out what fills your cup, keeps you ticking, and what makes you feel like the best version of yourself. Let's dive into how you can explore and find self-care strategies that resonate with you:

1. **Understanding Self-Care:**

   - Self-care includes anything that helps maintain your physical, mental, and emotional health. It can be as simple as getting enough sleep or as unique as your favorite hobby. It's all about what nurtures you personally.

2. **Identifying Personal Needs:**

   - Pause and reflect: What's throwing you off balance? Is it stress at work, physical tiredness, or feeling emotionally drained? Pinpointing where you need some TLC helps focus your self-care efforts.

3. **Exploring Self-Care Options:**

   - Dive into researching different ways to care for yourself. There's a world of ideas out there – from yoga and meditation to creative arts and nature walks. Keep an open mind and explore various options.

4. **Trying and Assessing:**

   - Start experimenting with different activities. Give meditation a go, try out a new exercise routine, or set aside time for reading. It's about trial and error – see what clicks and what doesn't. Give each activity some time and notice how you feel afterward.

5. **Tuning into Your Body and Mind:**

   - Listen to what your body and mind are telling you. Some activities might leave you feeling energized, while others might not hit the mark. It's all part of the journey. Keep notes on what lifts your spirits and what leaves you cold.

6. **Crafting Your Self-Care Routine:**

   - Once you've found what works, start building your personal self-care routine. Schedule these activities like any other important appointment. Regularity is key here – make self-care a consistent part of your day or week.

7. **Stay Flexible and Open to Change:**

   - Life changes, and so will your self-care needs. Be ready to adapt and tweak your routine. Maybe a new hobby catches your eye, or you outgrow a certain practice. Stay open to change and keep fine-tuning.

. . .

Remember, the quest for the perfect self-care routine is a personal and evolving journey. It's about finding what makes you feel refreshed, balanced, and ready to take on the world. Take the time to explore, listen to yourself, and most important, enjoy the process!

∾

CRAFTING A BALANCED LIFE: THE ART OF BOUNDARIES AND SELF-CARE

Getting your life in a groove where you feel balanced and content involves two key players: setting healthy boundaries and making self-care a daily thing. Let's break down how you can ace this balancing act:

1. **Figuring Out What You Need:**

   - Start by tuning into yourself. What gets you ticking? What calms you down? Recognize what you need for your physical, emotional, and mental well-being.

2. **Drawing the Line:**

   - Let those around you know what works for you and what doesn't. It's all about stating your limits clearly and kindly. Setting boundaries is like drawing a map that shows others how to treat you.

3. **The Power of 'No':**

- Saying 'no' can be tough, especially if you don't want to let others down. But remember, it's a key step in honoring your needs and limits. It's not about being unkind; it's about being fair to yourself.

4. **Scheduling in Self-Care:**

- Treat self-care like any other critical appointment. Whether it's a quiet coffee break, a brisk walk, or some time with a favorite book, make sure these moments are inked into your daily plan.

5. **Mindfulness and Relaxation:**

- Bring in some chill time every day. It could be through meditation, deep breathing, or even jotting down things you're grateful for. These practices can lower stress and clear your head.

6. **Balancing Work and Play:**

- Keep work within work hours. Once you clock out, focus on life outside the office. Also, try to keep a lid on endless screen scrolling. It's about giving your mind a break from constant digital buzz.

7. **Getting Backup:**

- Build a circle of pals or family who get your need for boundaries and self-care. They can be your cheer squad, keeping you on track and respecting your limits.

8. **Checking In with Yourself:**

- Regularly take stock of your routines and boundaries. Life changes, and so might your needs. Be open to tweaking your approach to keep things working for you.

. . .

Setting boundaries and focusing on self-care isn't about being self-centered. It's about ensuring you're in the best shape to tackle life head-on and be there for others when they need you. By looking after yourself, you're setting the stage for a happier, more balanced life where you can give your best to the world around you.

❧

BUILDING RESILIENCE: THE ROLE OF SELF-COMPASSION AND SELF-CARE

Resilience isn't just about toughing it out; it's about learning how to bounce back and keep going even when things get tough. And guess what? Self-compassion and self-care are your secret weapons in this journey. Here's how you can use them to build up your resilience:

1. **Self-Compassion: Your Inner Ally**

- Think of self-compassion as being your own best friend. It's about being kind to yourself, especially when you stumble or face tough times. Acknowledge nobody's perfect and that it's okay to have off days.
- Try this: When you're feeling down or critical of yourself, switch up your inner chat. Talk to yourself like you would to a good friend who's having a hard day. It's about changing the "I can't believe I messed up" to "Everyone makes mistakes, I'll learn from this."

2. **Self-Care: More Than Just Bubble Baths**

- Self-care isn't just about pampering; it's about taking care of
  your whole self. This means doing things that help you stay
  physically, mentally, and emotionally fit.
- What to do: Find activities that help you recharge. This could
  be anything from a quick walk, a healthy meal, to ensuring you
  get enough sleep. It's all about finding what helps you feel
  refreshed and balanced.

3. **Joy and Fulfillment: Feed Your Soul**

- Part of self-care is also doing things that make you happy and
  fulfilled. This could be anything from painting, gardening, to
  jamming on your guitar.
- The idea is to engage in activities that light you up inside. This
  not only boosts your mood but also builds emotional
  resilience.

4. **Consistency is Key**

- Remember, building resilience isn't a one-time thing; it's a
  continuous process. Make self-compassion and self-care a
  regular part of your life. They're not just for when you're
  feeling low; they're tools to keep you strong, no matter what
  life throws your way.

5. **Adapt and Adjust**

- Your needs will change over time, and that's normal. Regularly
  check in with yourself. Maybe what worked for you last year
  doesn't cut it now. Be open to tweaking your self-care routine
  to fit your current situation.
- Briefly, resilience is like a muscle - the more you work on it, the
  stronger it gets. And self-compassion and self-care are your

gym equipment. They help you build up the strength to face life's challenges with more ease and a lot more grace. So, start incorporating these practices into your life and watch how they transform your ability to handle whatever comes your way.

CULTIVATING SELF-COMPASSION AND SELF-CARE: NURTURING LIFELONG HABITS FOR WELL-BEING IN TOUGH TIMES

Life isn't always smooth sailing. We all go through rough patches that can knock us off our feet. But here's the thing: self-compassion and self-care aren't just fancy buzzwords. They're real tools that can help us handle these tough times better. They're about treating ourselves with the same kindness and understanding we'd offer a good friend. So, let's talk about how to weave these practices into our everyday lives and why they're game-changers for our overall well-being.

Understanding Self-Compassion: First off, self-compassion is like giving yourself a break. It's recognizing that it's okay not to be okay sometimes.

• **Mindfulness:** Try to be more aware of what you're feeling without getting too caught up in it. Practices like meditation or taking a moment to breathe can be a big help.

• **Kinder Self-Talk:** Cut out the harsh self-judgment. Instead, pep-talk yourself like you would your best mate. Positive affirmations can be a real boost.

Incorporating Self-Care into Daily Life: Self-care is all about doing things that make you feel good, both inside and out. It's not selfish; it's necessary.

• **Look After Your Body:** Eat well, get your beauty sleep, stay hydrated, and move your body in ways you enjoy.

• **Feed Your Soul:** Journal your thoughts, get creative, or just chat with someone who gets you. Remember to laugh and find joy in the little things.

Building Resilient Habits: Resilience isn't about never falling down; it's about getting back up again. And guess what? You can learn this skill.

• **Lean on Your Crew:** Share your worries with friends or family. Sometimes talking it out can make a huge difference.

• **Professional Support:** If things get too heavy, please talk with a therapist or counselor. They're pros at helping you navigate through tough times.

• **Be Flexible:** Life's all about change, so try to roll with the punches. Adapting to new situations can turn challenges into opportunities for growth.

Conclusion: Making self-compassion and self-care part of your daily routine isn't just a good idea; it's essential for riding out life's storms. These practices help us stay grounded, keep things in perspective, and remind us that it's okay to put ourselves first sometimes. By focusing on our well-being, we're not just surviving; we're thriving, no matter what life throws our way.

SECTION NINE WRAP-UP:

KEY POINTS:

SELF-COMPASSION: Your Inner Ally

- **Understanding Self-Compassion:** Treat yourself with kindness and empathy, especially during tough times.
- **Importance of Self-Compassion:** Helps manage difficult emotions, reduces self-criticism, and fosters inner peace.
- **Changing the Inner Dialogue:** Shift from self-criticism to a supportive and understanding inner voice.

Self-Care: Recharging Your Batteries

- **Essence of Self-Care:** Engaging in activities that replenish energy, reduce stress, and maintain overall well-being.
- **Busting Self-Care Myths:** Recognize self-care as essential, not selfish or secondary.
- **Self-Care Activities:** Find activities that bring you joy and peace, and make them a regular part of your life.

Why Self-Care and Self-Compassion Are Essential

- **Like an Oxygen Mask:** Prioritize self-care to effectively help others.
- **Benefits Beyond Personal:** Enhances emotional resilience and improves your ability to support others.

ACTION ITEMS:

Fostering Self-Compassion

- **Monitor Self-Talk:** Pay attention to your internal dialogue. Replace negative or harsh thoughts with kinder, more supportive ones.
- **Practice Mindfulness:** Be present in the moment and acknowledge your feelings without judgment.
- **Write Affirmations:** Create positive affirmations that reinforce self-compassion and repeat them daily.

Implementing Self-Care

- **Identify Self-Care Activities:** Make a list of activities that help you relax and recharge, like exercise, hobbies, or spending time with loved ones.
- **Create a Self-Care Schedule:** Allocate specific times in your routine for self-care activities.
- **Reflect on Self-Care:** Regularly assess how your self-care activities are affecting your well-being and adjust as needed.

Enhancing Overall Well-being

- **Seek Support:** Talk to friends, family, or professionals about your feelings and challenges.
- **Learn and Grow from Challenges:** Reflect on your challenges and what you can learn from them.

- **Stay Flexible:** Be open to changing your self-care strategies as your needs evolve.

In Our Next Section:

In our next section, we'll dig into the art of building and nurturing relationships, both personal and professional. Relationships are the bedrock of our lives, offering support, inspiration, and collaboration opportunities. Whether you're fostering friendships, deepening family ties, or strengthening work connections, each relationship adds unique value to your journey.

We'll explore practical strategies for creating meaningful interactions, maintaining healthy communication, and resolving conflicts constructively. You'll learn how to cultivate a network of supportive and diverse connections that enrich your life and career. Embracing these insights will not only enhance your interpersonal skills but also empower you to create a circle of influence marked by trust, respect, and mutual growth. So, gear up to unlock the power of relationships, transforming every interaction into a stepping stone toward personal fulfillment and professional success.

SECTION TEN: EMBRACING CHANGE AS AN OPPORTUNITY FOR GROWTH:

NAVIGATING THE TIDES OF CHANGE

CHANGE IS a bit like the weather – always happening and out of our control. From the second we're born, we're on this rollercoaster ride in a world that's always moving and shaking. It's just part of the gig of being alive, and the sooner we get comfy with it, the better we can ride those waves.

Let's break it down:

- **Change Comes in All Sizes:** Life throws different kinds of change at us. Some are big game-changers, others might seem tiny, but they all count. Each has the power to shape us, teach us, and push us to grow, both personally and professionally.
- **Personal Growth and Change:** Personal growth often happens when change nudges us out of our cozy comfort zones. Think about it – moving to a new place or starting a new gig can stretch your independence muscles. Tough times like breakups or losing someone can be rough, but they also make you wiser and stronger.
- **Professional Growth Loves Change:** In the work world, everything's always on the move – new tech, new trends, you name it. To keep up and not get left behind, we've got to be like

chameleons – always ready to learn new tricks and adapt. Sticking to the old ways? That's a one-way ticket to Stagnant City.

- **Change Can Be Sneaky:** Sometimes, change is slow and steady, and other times it's like a surprise party you didn't see coming. The key is to keep your eyes peeled and stay ready, so you're not thrown off balance when it happens.
- **Embrace the Change:** Here's the fun part – change is actually packed with opportunities. It dares us to step up, try new things, and shake up the usual routine. Welcoming change is like saying yes to growth, learning, and improving at life and work.

Briefly, change is a big deal in the grand story of our lives. It molds us, challenges us, and opens doors to new adventures. By accepting and rolling with change, we set ourselves up for a journey all about growing, learning, and becoming the best versions of ourselves. So, let's get ready to embrace change and all the awesome stuff it brings!

EMBRACING CHANGE: A PATH TO GROWTH AND RESILIENCE

CHANGE. It is inevitable, whether we like it or not. It is an ever-present force that shapes our lives and pushes us toward new and uncharted territories. Yet, many of us approach change with fear and trepidation, desperately clinging to the comfort of our familiar routines. What if we were to reframe our perspective and see change as an opportunity for growth and self-improvement? In this chapter, we will explore the significance of adopting a positive and open mindset toward change. We will dig into the transformative power of embracing change, and how it can lead us on a path of personal development, resilience, and overcoming challenges.

Part 1: Recognizing the Impacts of a Closed Mindset

Let's talk about something that's a big deal in our lives: change. It's everywhere, right? But a lot of us are hesitant about it. We're comfortable in our cozy little routines, and the thought of stepping into the unknown can be kinda scary. So, what's up with that?

1.1 The Unknown - Why We're Hesitant:

• **Why Change Scares Us:** This fear of what we don't know is deep-seated. Think about it. Back in the day, our ancestors had to be cautious. Taking risks could mean trouble. So, they passed down this careful nature to us. Fast forward to today, and here we are, still wary of the unfamiliar. It's like our brains are hardwired to prefer the known over the unknown, because hey, better safe than sorry, right?

1.2 Stuck in a Rut - When We Don't Embrace Change:

• **Missing Out Big Time:** Now, when we're all about that 'no-change' life, we miss out on a bunch of stuff. Think personal growth, new opportunities, the whole shebang. Sticking to what we know feels safe, but it's also like putting on blinders. We don't see the cool stuff that could come from trying something different. And working with others? Forget about it. If we're not open to new ideas, teamwork becomes a tough nut to crack.

1.3 Change and Our Mindset:

• **How We Think Matters:** So, it turns out the way we think about change matters. If we think we can't change, guess what? We probably won't. But if we believe we can grow and learn, that's when the magic happens. We start seeing challenges as chances to improve, not just scary roadblocks.

• **Fixed vs. Growth:** People with a fixed mindset are like, "This is how I am, and that's that." They avoid challenges like the plague. But then there's the growth mindset gang. They're all about learning and improving. They see challenges as a chance to level up in life.

• **Switching Gears to Growth:** The cool part? We can change our mindset. It's all about embracing challenges, focusing on the journey, not just the destination, and bouncing back from setbacks. Plus, surrounding ourselves with positive, growth-minded folks can help.

• **Learning Never Stops:** Keeping that brain of ours hungry for new stuff and experiences is key. Workshops, books, just being curious – this keeps our mindset in growth mode.

So, what's the takeaway? Change is a big part of life. It can be scary, sure. But by shifting our mindset and seeing it as a chance to grow, we can turn the scary into something awesome. It's all about learning, staying open to new ideas, and remembering that it's okay to stumble along the way. Let's embrace the change and see where it takes us!

Part 2: Tapping into Open Mindset Power for Creative Wins and Learning

2.1 Flipping the Switch to Growth Mode in the Face of Change:

• **Change = Learning:** Hey, change is part of the game. It can throw us curveballs, but guess what? It's also packed with chances to learn and grow. If we play it right, change becomes less of a scary monster and more of a cool teacher.

• **Growth Mindset 101:** It's all about believing we can improve at stuff. Think of it like a muscle - the more you use it, the stronger it gets. Embracing change? That's like a workout for your brain.

• **Staying Open and Curious:** When change is knocking, open the door! Get comfortable with being uncomfortable. It's all part of the deal when you're growing and learning.

• **Learning from Others:** Don't go at it alone. Chat with folks who've been there, done that. They might have the golden advice you need.

• **Reflecting on Past Wins:** Remember that time you nailed it? That wasn't a fluke. Look back at your successes for a confidence boost.

• **Effort Over Perfection:** It's not about nailing it every time. It's about trying, messing up, learning, and trying again. That's where the real growth happens.

• **Stay Curious:** Keep that spark of curiosity alive. It's the fuel for your growth engine.

2.2 Building Bounce-Back Power: How to Keep Going When It Gets Tough:

• **Growth Mindset, Again:** Yep, it's back. Seeing challenges as chances to improve helps us keep pushing, even when the going gets tough.

• **Know Yourself:** Understanding how you tick can make a world of difference. Reflect on your reactions and learn from them.

• **Mindfulness Matters:** Take a breath. Focus on the now. It's a game-changer when stress levels are off the charts.

• **Your Crew Counts:** Having people who've got your back makes all the difference. Share, listen, and support each other.

• **Set Goals That Make Sense:** Bite-sized goals can lead to giant leaps. Tackle the small stuff and watch how it adds up.

• **Take Care of You:** Rest, hobbies, joy - they're not just nice-to-haves. They're essential for keeping you in top shape to face those challenges.

• **Celebrate the Little Things:** Every step forward is worth a high five. Recognize your progress and let it fuel you for the next round.

2.3 Opening the Doors to Creativity and Innovation:

• **What's an Open Mindset?** It's about welcoming new ideas and perspectives. Think of it as a big "Welcome!" sign for fresh thoughts and experiences.

• **Curiosity is Key:** Ask questions, explore, and keep that sense of wonder alive. It's the secret sauce for creative thinking.

• **Break Free from the Same Old:** Challenge what you think you know. New angles can lead to amazing discoveries.

• **Failures Are Gold:** They're not just bumps in the road; they're learning opportunities. Each misstep teaches us something new.

• **Diversity Drives Innovation:** Different voices and viewpoints? They're not just nice; they're necessary. They bring in the kind of thinking that can change the game.

• **Walk in Others' Shoes:** Understanding people's needs and experiences opens up whole new worlds of ideas.

• **Never Stop Learning:** The world's always changing, and so should we. Keep learning, growing, and expanding your mind.

• **To Sum It Up:** Keeping an open mind isn't just about being nice. It's about unlocking your full creative potential. It's about seeing the world in vibrant colors and endless possibilities. So, let's stay open, curious, and ready to embrace the new. Let's make magic happen!

Part 3: Navigating Change for Self-Improvement

3.1 Mirror Time: Knowing Your Strengths and Where to Grow:

• **Know Yourself:** It's all about taking a good, hard look at yourself. Figure out what you're great at and where you could use a little polish. For example, I'm a champ at organizing and problem-solving, but hey, I'm working on beefing up my self-confidence and juggling my time better.

• **Celebrate Strengths:** Own your strong points! Whether it's being a communication wizard or a master planner, these are your superpowers. Use them well.

• **Face Growth Areas:** We've all got them – those areas where we're not quite superheroes yet. For me, it's about cranking up that self-belief and getting sharper at time management. The trick is to face these areas head-on and get to work on them.

3.2 Getting Out There: Embracing New Experiences:

• **Comfort Zone? Bye-Bye:** Sticking to what you know is cozy, but the real magic happens when you step out into the unknown. It's scary but oh-so rewarding.

• **Ride the Wave of Change:** See change as this big, exciting wave you can surf on, not something to run from. It's about growth, learning, and finding your potential.

• **Small Steps, Big Leaps:** Start small. Test the waters with little challenges and build up from there. Every tiny step outside your comfort zone is a win.

• **Fear? More Like a Friend:** Fear's not your enemy; it's a sign you're onto something good. Shake hands with it and use it as a signpost to something great.

3.3 Your People, Your Power: Building a Support Network for Change:

• **Why Support Rocks:** Going through change is way easier when you've got folks to lean on. A support network can be your sounding board, your cheer squad, and your brainstorming crew all rolled into one.

• **Mix It Up:** Your support network should be as diverse as a party mix. Think friends, colleagues, mentors, and even online communities.

• **The Power of Sharing:** Got worries or challenges? Don't keep them bottled up. Share them with your network. You'll get fresh perspectives, advice, and maybe a pep talk or two.

• **Give as Good as You Get:** Remember, it's a two-way street. Help out others in your network, too. Share your skills, lend an ear, and be a pal.

• **Learning Together:** Embrace the idea of learning with and from your network. Swap stories, skills, and experiences. It's like a buffet of knowledge and support.

To Wrap It Up:

• **Self-Reflection:** Dive deep into knowing your strengths and areas for growth. It's like a personal treasure hunt.

• **Embrace the New:** Get comfy with being a little uncomfy. New experiences are where you grow.

• **Build Your Squad:** Surround yourself with people who lift you up and push you forward. They're your secret weapon in the world of change.

Part 4: Navigating Life's Hurdles

4.1 Dealing with the Unknown: Mastering the Art of Uncertainty

• **Tackling Uncertainty:** Life's full of surprises, and not knowing what's next can be daunting. But, there's a trick to getting through it: embracing uncertainty as a normal part of life and learning how to roll with it.

• **Skills for the Unpredictable:** It's about picking up skills that help you stay cool and make smart moves, even when things are up in the air. Think adaptability, problem-solving, and keeping a clear head.

4.2 Turning Setbacks into Comebacks: Learning from Failure

• **Rethinking Failure:** Sure, nobody likes to fail. But what if we saw it as just a pit stop on the road to success? Every time things don't go as planned, there's a chance to learn something valuable.

• **Learning from the Lows:** It's about looking closely at what went wrong, figuring out the lessons, and using them to come back stronger. Remember, the most successful people are often those who've bounced back from a few knocks.

4.3 Spotting the Silver Lining: Finding Opportunities in Challenges

• **Change as a Chance to Grow:** When life throws a curveball, instead of ducking, think about how you can hit it out of the park. It's all about finding that silver lining and turning challenges into opportunities.

• **Embracing the New:** Got tossed into unfamiliar territory? Great! It's the perfect time to learn new skills, rethink your goals, and maybe even discover a new passion.

• **Resilience is Key:** Tough times can test you. But they're also prime time for building resilience. The more you flex that muscle, the stronger you get at handling whatever life throws at you.

Conclusion:

• **Change is Your Friend:** So, here's the takeaway: change isn't something to fear. It's an opportunity to grow, learn, and become the best version of yourself. With the right mindset, a willingness to learn, and grit, you can turn even the trickiest situations into steppingstones for success. Let's embrace change and make it work for us!

NAVIGATING THE UNCOMFORTABLE SIDE OF CHANGE

LET'S BE REAL – change can be as uncomfortable as wearing a sweater that's too tight. It messes with our usual flow, pushes us into new places, and can be downright scary. But guess what? It's also where the magic of growth happens. So, let's talk about why stepping out of our comfort zone is the secret sauce to personal growth and how to handle it like a pro.

• **Breaking Free from Self-Imposed Limits:** Our comfort zones are cozy but can sometimes feel like invisible fences holding us back. By daring to step beyond these boundaries, we open ourselves up to new experiences, ideas, and a whole world of possibilities we might have missed out on if we played it safe.

• **Building Resilience and Adaptability:** Life's like a river – always moving, always changing. When we voluntarily dive into new and challenging situations, we're basically training ourselves to swim in these ever-changing waters. We get better at dealing with setbacks, adapting to new environments, and picking ourselves up after a tumble.

But hey, embracing discomfort doesn't mean you throw caution to the wind. Here's how to smartly navigate these waters:

• **Recognize and Accept the Feels:** Feeling uncomfortable? That's normal. Instead of running from it, acknowledge it. It's a part of the change process, like a rite of passage to growth.

• **Baby Steps to Big Leaps:** You need not jump off the deep end right away. Start small, set achievable goals, and gradually expand your comfort zone. Celebrate those little wins – they add up!

• **Lean on Your Squad:** Having a supportive crew can make a world of difference. They're your cheerleaders, advisors, and sounding boards. Don't hesitate to reach out for a pep talk or a piece of wisdom.

• **Eyes on the Prize:** Keep in mind why you're stepping out of your comfort zone in the first place. Focus on the big picture – your goals, dreams, and the person you're aiming to become. This perspective can be the light guiding you through the uncomfortable moments.

Briefly, while change might be uncomfortable, it's also where you grow, learn, and discover your awesomeness. It's about challenging yourself, building your resilience muscle, and ultimately, shaping a life that's rich, fulfilling, and so very you. So, embrace the discomfort, take it one step at a time, and watch yourself flourish in the face of change.

RIDING THE WAVE OF LIFE'S TRANSITIONS

CHANGE – it's like the weather, always happening and sometimes unpredictable. Life throws us into new scenes all the time, be it a fresh job, a new relationship, or even a change in where we call home. Sure, these shifts can be thrilling and open up doors we never knew existed, but let's not sugarcoat it – they can also be a real test of our mettle. Let's dive into some savvy ways to tackle these transitions and come out stronger on the other side.

Embracing Flexibility: The Art of Going with the Flow

Regarding transitions, being flexible is like having a secret superpower. Here's how to flex those flexibility muscles:

• **Embrace Uncertainty:** Look at uncertainty not as a giant question mark looming over your head, but as a blank canvas waiting for your masterpiece. It's a chance to grow and reinvent yourself.

• **Open-mindedness:** Keep an open mind like an open door – welcoming new ideas and experiences. This mindset can turn even the bumpiest transitions into smoother rides.

• **Let Go of Expectations:** Sometimes, we need to unclasp those tight fists of expectation. Be ready to tweak, adjust, and sometimes overhaul your initial plans. Rigidity can be a roadblock to success.

Building Resilience: Your Comeback Toolkit

Bouncing back from tough times is all about resilience. Here's how to build yours:

• **Growth Mindset:** View challenges not as dead ends, but as stepping-stones. Every hiccup is a lesson in disguise.

• **Strong Support System:** Rally your personal cheer squad. Friends, family, mentors – these are your go-to people when the going gets tough.

• **Self-Care:** Remember, you can't pour from an empty cup. Whether it's a jog in the park, meditation, or just some downtime with a good book, make sure you're recharging those batteries.

Fostering Adaptability: Becoming a Change Champion

Adaptability is like being a chameleon, but in life. Here's how to master it:

• **Change as an Opportunity:** Instead of resisting change, try to see it as the universe handing you a golden ticket to new adventures.

• **Continuous Learning:** Keep your brain hungry for new knowledge and skills. Staying curious and open to learning keeps you nimble and ready for anything.

• **Reflect and Adjust:** Regularly step back, reflect on your journey, and tweak your sails. Staying adaptable means being ready to make changes as you go.

Chapter Conclusion: Navigating Life's Waters

So there you have it. Life's transitions, while challenging, are also ripe with opportunity. By keeping flexible, resilient, and adaptable, you're not just surviving these changes – you're thriving through them. Embrace the new, learn from the setbacks, and remember, every transition is a chance to write a new chapter in your story. Ready to turn the page? Let's do this!

TURNING CHANGE INTO A MIRROR: THE ART OF CULTIVATING SELF-AWARENESS

Change, big or small, is a constant companion in our lives. Think of it like a river, constantly flowing, sometimes calm, sometimes wild. Whether it's a major life event like switching careers or something smaller like changing your morning routine, these shifts often prompt us to pause and ponder – who are we, and where are we going? This is where the magic of self-awareness comes into play.

The Deep Dive of Introspection

When life shakes up our regular programming, it's like getting an invite to take a deep dive into ourselves. This introspection, the act of exploring our inner universe, can be quite the eye-opener. It's like holding up a mirror to our thoughts, feelings, and experiences, asking, "Hey, what's really going on in there?" This self-reflection can reveal our true strengths, our hidden fears, even passions we didn't know we had.

Confronting the Unfamiliar

Change has a way of nudging us out of our cozy nests. Suddenly, we're asking ourselves hard questions, reassessing our values, and wondering what we want out of life. This self-interrogation isn't always comfortable, but it's necessary for growth. It's like shedding an old skin to make way for something new and more fitting.

New Perspectives and Personal Growth

Stepping into unknown territories – be it a new city, job, or social circle – exposes us to different people and ideas. It's like adding new colors to our personal palette, enriching us, and making us more adaptable. Plus, overcoming the challenges that come with change? That's a sure-fire way to boost our self-confidence.

Self-Reflection: A Path to a More Authentic Life

Change isn't just about what's happening around us; it's about what's happening within us. By reflecting on our inner selves, we can pinpoint what needs tweaking, set meaningful goals, and stride toward a more satisfying and authentic existence.

Chapter Conclusion: Embracing Change as a Catalyst

Briefly, change isn't just something that happens to us – it's a chance for us to happen to ourselves. It's a golden opportunity for self-discovery and growth. By welcoming change with open arms and a reflective mind, we start a fascinating journey of self-awareness, leading to a life that's not just lived but truly experienced. So, let's raise a glass to change – the unexpected teacher, the mirror that shows us who we are.

∾

NAVIGATING LIFE'S CHANGES WITH A SUPPORT SYSTEM

Life's like a river – always flowing, sometimes calm, sometimes turbulent. And when the waters get choppy, like during a big career shift or moving to a new city, it's easy to feel lost at sea. That's where having a solid support system comes in – think of it as your life raft.

The Power of Support: More Than Just a Safety Net

A strong support network – friends, family, mentors – can be a game-changer during times of change. They're the folks who give you a pep talk, lend an ear, and offer a shoulder to lean on. Their presence is like a beacon of light in the fog, guiding you through uncharted waters with more confidence.

Why a Good Support Crew Matters

• **Boosting Your Confidence**: Your support circle is like your personal cheer squad. They see the best in you, even when you're doubting yourself. They're the ones nudging you to leap into new experiences, reassuring you that you've got what it takes.

• **Sharing Wisdom**: They're like your personal library of life experiences. They've been there, done that, and their insights can be pure gold, helping you avoid pitfalls and make smarter choices.

• **Keeping You on Track**: Ever feel like you're veering off course? That's where your support team comes in. They're your accountability partners, keeping you focused and cheering you on every step of the way.

• **Celebrating the Wins**: Every milestone, no matter how small, is worth celebrating, and your support network is there to pop the champagne and toast to your successes.

Asking for Help: A Sign of Strength, Not Weakness

Reaching out for support isn't waving a white flag; it's a smart move. It shows you're wise enough to know when you need guidance and strong enough to ask for it. It's about embracing our shared human experience and understanding that we're all in this together.

Building Your Support System: A Worthwhile Endeavor

Cultivating a strong support system is a bit like planting a garden. It takes time, care, and effort. Look for people who get you, offer sound advice, and stand by you through thick and thin. These relationships are precious and worth every bit of effort you put into them.

Chapter Conclusion: Embracing Change with a Little Help from Our Friends

Life's changes can be daunting, but with a solid support system by your side, you're never going it alone. They're your sounding board, your reality check, and your cheerleaders, all rolled into one. So let's not be shy about leaning on our support network. After all, they're one of our greatest assets in navigating the ever-changing tides of life.

HARNESSING CHANGE FOR PERSONAL GROWTH

ALL RIGHT, let's wrap up our chat about change. This part is like the cherry on top. It's about grabbing change by the horns and using it to grow and get ahead. We've talked a lot, and now it's about putting all that into action. It's about getting good at dealing with change and even making the most out of it.

Embracing Change: First things first, we've got to get comfy with change. It's like that friend who always pops by unannounced – you might as well get used to it! Instead of pushing back or freaking out, try to be open and go with the flow. Change is just how life rolls, and when you're cool with it, all that stress and worry takes a backseat. Being flexible means, you can handle whatever life throws your way.

Spotting Opportunities: Change is sneaky – it often brings goodies in disguise. These could be a fresh project at work, bumping into someone who can open doors for you, or a surprise turn in your personal life. The trick is to keep your eyes peeled and jump on these chances. Yeah, it takes guts and you might need to step out of your safe zone, but that's how you grow. Each chance you take is a step up in your personal journey.

Learning from Experiences: Every change, whether it's a high or a low, is a chance to learn. Think of it as going to the school of life. Reflecting on what's happened helps you pick up lessons, tweak your game plan, and make smarter moves next time. This is how you get wise, see things in new ways, and toughen up. Learning from what life throws at you is what shapes you into a well-rounded person.

Practical Strategies: Now, how do you actually make all this happen? It's about regularly checking in with yourself, getting feedback from people you trust, and always aiming to grow. When you reflect on your own, you get to know yourself better – what you're good at and what you could work on. Feedback from others can show you things you might not see yourself. And that growth mindset? That's about not giving up when things get tough and seeing every flop as a chance to learn.

Wrapping It Up: So, there you have it. By getting on board with change, grabbing chances, and learning from everything, change becomes a tool for your personal growth. This last bit is all about encouraging you to be open to change, chase opportunities, and always be hungry for learning and growing. With these tricks up your sleeve, you can make the most of this ever-changing world and shine.

SECTION TEN WRAP-UP:

EMBRACING Change as an Opportunity for Growth

• **Change is Inevitable:** Recognize that change, big or small, is a constant in life.

• **Personal and Professional Growth:** Use change as a catalyst for growth in all areas of your life.

• **Unexpected Opportunities:** View change as a source of new possibilities and experiences.

• **Continuous Learning:** Adapt and evolve by staying open to learning from every situation.

• **Resilience Through Change:** Build resilience by using change as a tool to become stronger and more adaptable.

ACTION ITEMS:

• **Assess Your Attitude Toward Change:** Take time to reflect on how you typically respond to change. Are you resistant, fearful, or welcoming?

• **Develop a Growth Mindset:** Cultivate an attitude where you see challenges and changes as opportunities to learn and grow.

• **Stay Informed and Flexible:** Keep abreast of changes in your industry or personal life and be ready to adapt your strategies.

• **Practice Reflective Learning:** After each significant change, reflect on what you learned and how you can apply this knowledge.

• **Seek Support When Needed:** Don't hesitate to reach out to your network for advice and support during times of change.

• **Embrace New Opportunities:** Actively look for and seize new opportunities that arise from changes in your environment.

• **Prioritize Self-Care:** Ensure you are taking care of your physical and mental health during periods of change.

By embracing these key points and action items, you can turn the challenges of change into steppingstones for personal and professional development, leading to a more fulfilling and resilient life.

In Our Next Section:

In our next section, we'll start a journey of self-discovery and personal mastery. We will explore the transformative power of self-awareness and self-improvement. It's about diving deep into who we are, understanding our unique strengths and areas where we can grow. We'll uncover how self-awareness is not just about introspection; it's a powerful tool for shaping our responses to the world around us, enhancing our relationships, and guiding our personal and professional growth.

As we dig into the art of self-improvement, we'll discover practical, actionable strategies to help us evolve and adapt in a constantly changing world. You'll learn how to set meaningful goals, develop new skills, and cultivate a mindset geared toward continuous growth. This section is designed to motivate and inspire you to take control of your personal development journey. It's about recognizing that every day presents an opportunity to learn something new about ourselves and the world, transforming challenges into steppingstones toward a more fulfilled and successful life. Let's get ready to unlock our potential and turn aspirations into reality!

SECTION ELEVEN: MAINTAINING A POSITIVE MINDSET IN THE FACE OF CHALLENGES

HARNESSING THE POWER OF
A POSITIVE MINDSET

LET'S chat about the magic of having a positive mindset. It's like this secret superpower that can make a difference in how we tackle life's hurdles and enjoy the ride. When we look at things through a "glass-half-full" lens, it changes the game – we become more determined, find better solutions, and, hey, we might even end up happier and more successful.

The Resilience Factor: With a positive mindset, you're like a bounce-back champion. Challenges? You see them as steppingstones, not stop signs. This attitude means you don't get bogged down when things get tough. Instead, you're all about pushing through, learning, and growing. It turns the whole "problem" thing into something more manageable and, believe it or not, even exciting.

Learning from the Lows: Nobody's perfect, and we all face setbacks. But here's where a positive mindset shines. Instead of stewing over what went wrong, it's about digging out the lessons from those not-so-great moments. This way, every stumble becomes a chance to level up and come back stronger.

Gratitude and Appreciation: A positive mindset isn't just about dealing with the tough stuff. It's also about enjoying the good stuff –

like recognizing your strengths, celebrating wins, and cherishing the people who have your back. This gratitude attitude keeps the spirits high and stress low.

Attracting Good Vibes: Ever notice how positive people seem to attract good things? That's because confidence, hope, and enthusiasm are contagious. With a positive mindset, you're more likely to jump on new opportunities, take a few risks, and meet people who can open doors. It's like a magnet for cool possibilities and connections.

Mind and Body Wellness: Thinking positive doesn't just feel good – it's actually good for you. Studies show that folks with a sunny outlook have less stress, lower chances of feeling down, and even better physical health. It's like a wellness booster shot for both your mind and body.

Wrap-Up: So, briefly, a positive mindset is a total game-changer. It helps you deal with challenges, learn from your lows, appreciate the now, attract good things, and keep yourself healthy and happy. It's about seeing life as a glass half full – and sometimes, that's all it takes to make a world of difference.

TURNING NEGATIVE THOUGHTS INTO POSITIVE VIBES

ALL RIGHT LET'S talk about flipping the script on those pesky negative thoughts. You know, the ones that sneak up on us and throw a wrench in our day. Here's the deal – by recognizing and tweaking these thoughts, we can boost our mental game and get a sunnier outlook on life. Here's how:

Mindful Moments: First up, let's get our mindfulness game on. It's all about tuning into your thoughts. Feel a gloomy thought creeping in? Acknowledge it, but don't invite it to stay for dinner. Catching these thoughts early is key.

Challenge the Negative: Next, put on your detective hat and question those negative thoughts. Are they really true, or just sneaky little lies? Often, they're just irrational beliefs. Swap them out with thoughts that are more logical and kinder to yourself.

Reframe the Game: Got a negative thought? Let's give it a makeover. For example, change "I'm not cut out for this" to "Hey, I've got skills and I'm ready to learn." It's about finding the silver lining in every cloud.

Positive Pep-Talk: Create a go-to list of feel-good affirmations. Find ones that speak to you and echo your goals. Say them out loud, in your head, or write them down – whatever works for you. They're like little cheerleaders for your self-esteem.

Surround Yourself with Sunshine: Be mindful of who and what you let into your world. Choose friends who lift you up, stories that inspire, and places that give you good vibes. It's like setting up your personal positivity bubble.

Gratitude Attitude: Jump on the gratitude train. Every day, jot down a few things you're thankful for. It shifts your focus from "what's wrong" to "what's right," and that's a game-changer.

Lean on Your Squad: When the going gets tough, reach out to your people. Talk it out with friends, family, or even a therapist. Sometimes, just airing it out can lighten the load, and they might offer fresh, helpful perspectives.

Self-Care Rituals: Don't forget to take care of you. Exercise, eat well, get your Z's, and dive into hobbies that make your heart sing. When you're good to yourself, you lay the groundwork for more positive thoughts.

Remember, Rome wasn't built in a day, and neither is a positive mind-set. Give yourself some grace and keep at it. Bit by bit, you'll see those negative thoughts turn into positive ones, and that's when the real magic happens. Keep going – you got this!

BUILDING YOUR RESILIENCE AND KEEPIN' ON KEEPING ON

Building Your Resilience and Keepin' On Keeping On

Let's chat about resilience – that superpower that lets you take life's punches and still stand strong. It's not just about toughing it out, but about learning how to dance in the rain, you know? Here's the lowdown on beefing up your resilience and keeping your head up, no matter what.

Life's Hurdles: Just Learning Opportunities in Disguise First things first, let's flip the script on setbacks. Instead of seeing them as downers, think of them as your personal trainers for growth. With a growth mindset, every challenge is a chance to level up. It's all about evolving and improving every day.

Stay Positive, Stay Strong Keeping a positive vibe is key. This doesn't mean you ignore the rough stuff. It's about facing those tough emotions, then finding a way to spin them into something constructive. A sprinkle of gratitude goes a long way, too. Focusing on the good stuff can keep your spirits high.

Your Squad Matters Having a tribe that's got your back is priceless. Surround yourself with folks who lift you up and offer solid advice when the going gets tough. And remember, it's a two-way street – be there for them, too. Strong bonds make for a solid support system.

Keep Calm and Carry On Managing your emotions is important. Practices like mindfulness or meditation can be game-changers. They help you stay chill and think clearly when life throws a curveball. And hey, don't forget to break a sweat! Exercise is a great stress-buster and mood-lifter.

Problem-Solving Like a Boss Focus on solutions, not problems. Break big challenges into bite-sized pieces. Set small goals that lead to big victories. This keeps you moving forward and keeps your motivation tank full.

Self-Care Isn't Selfish Taking care of yourself is important. Get enough sleep, eat right, and find time for things that make you happy. Whether it's jamming on a guitar or chilling in a hammock, do more of what makes your heart sing.

So, there you have it. Building resilience is about seeing challenges as chances to grow, staying upbeat, leaning on and supporting others, managing stress, tackling problems head-on, and looking after yourself. Keep working on these, and you'll be amazed at how much you can handle. Remember, resilience is a journey, not a destination, so enjoy the ride!

SOAKING UP THE GOOD VIBES: THE MAGIC OF POSITIVE INFLUENCES

All right let's talk about the powerhouse move of wrapping yourself up in positivity. It's like this secret weapon for keeping your spirits high and your mindset right. Whether it's chillin' with friends who lift you up, finding mentors who inspire, or soaking in all the good stuff from books and podcasts, positive vibes play a big role in how you see the world and tackle life's challenges.

Friends Who Are Like Sunshine First off, having friends who sprinkle positivity is like having your personal cheer squad. These are the folks who see the real you, push you toward your dreams, and have your back no matter what. They're the ones turning your 'I can't' into 'I can', and your 'I won't' into 'I will'. They listen, they get it, and they keep you grounded and soaring at the same time. With these gems in your life, you're more likely to feel confident and see the brighter side of things.

Mentors: Your Personal Life Coaches Then there's the magic of mentors. These are the people who've walked the path and have the scars and stories to prove it. They're the wise wizards of life – offering nuggets of wisdom, new perspectives, and that little nudge when you need it. Having someone who's got faith in your potential is a game-changer. It's like having a personal life coach who's rooting for you and shows you the ropes.

Fill Your Feed with Feel-Good And let's not forget the power of inspiring content. Whether it's a book that opens new worlds for you, a podcast that lights a fire in your belly, or social media feeds that are all about the good vibes – what you consume matters big time. This stuff shapes your thoughts, molds your perspectives, and can turn a meh day into a 'heck yeah' day. It's about feeding your mind with the kind of fuel that keeps you going strong.

Wrapping it up, surrounding yourself with positivity is like building your own personal fortress of good vibes. It's about having friends who are your cheerleaders, mentors who guide you, and content that keeps you inspired. This combo is your ticket to a mindset all about growth, gratitude, and getting after your goals. So, build that positive bubble – it's your secret sauce for a happy, fulfilling life.

∾

PRACTICING GRATITUDE AND MINDFULNESS:

Practicing gratitude and mindfulness are like superfoods for your brain and heart. They help you feel more upbeat, satisfied, and centered. Here's the lowdown on their perks and how to make them a regular part of your life:

Perks of Gratitude:

• **Boosts Your Mood:** Acknowledging the good stuff in life can lift your spirits.

• **Better Mental Health:** Regularly feeling thankful can help keep stress, anxiety, and the blues at bay.

• **Stronger Relationships:** Saying thanks to people not only makes them feel good, but it also strengthens your bond with them.

• **Sees the Glass Half Full:** Focusing on what you've got, rather than what you don't, trains your brain to see the bright side.

Perks of Mindfulness:

• **Less Stress:** Being mindful helps you take a chill pill when things get hectic.

• **Sharper Focus:** Regularly tuning into the moment can sharpen your concentration and make you more productive.

• **Handles Emotions Like a Pro:** By watching your feelings without judgment, you get better at managing how you react to them.

• **Kind to Yourself:** Mindfulness boosts your self-love and self-respect, giving you a healthier self-image.

How to Make Them Part of Your Life:

1. **Gratitude Journal:** Every day, jot down three things that made you feel grateful. Could be as simple as your morning latte or a friend's text.

2. **Say Thank You:** Show gratitude in your day-to-day interactions. A little thanks can go a long way.

3. **Mindful Breathing:** Take out a few minutes for some mindful breathing. Focus on your breath, bring yourself to the here and now, and just let go of any stress.

4. **Mindful Eating:** When eating, focus on the experience. Enjoy the taste, aroma, and feel of your food.

5. **Body Scan Meditation:** Spend a few minutes scanning your body, head to toe. Notice any tension and breathe into it to help relax.

6. **Gratitude Walk:** Go for a walk and take in your surroundings. Appreciate everything, from the chirping birds to the rustling leaves.

Remember, like learning to ride a bike, getting good at gratitude and mindfulness takes practice. Stick with it, and soon enough, you'll be reaping the feel-good rewards.

EMBRACING FAILURE: THE PATH TO GROWTH AND STRENGTH

In life, we're bound to face setbacks and failures. The real magic lies in how we respond to these bumps in the road. Instead of seeing them as dead ends, it's way more helpful to look at them as invaluable chances to grow. Let's dive into how we can flip the script on failures and use them as launchpads for success.

Growth Mindset is Key: Think of a growth mindset as your secret weapon. It's all about understanding you can develop your skills and talents with effort and persistence. Don't let failure define you. See it as just a pitstop, not the end of the road. Every mistake is an opportunity to learn and improve.

Reflect and Analyze: When things don't go as planned, step back. What went sideways? Why? Dig into the details and be brutally honest with yourself. This isn't about beating yourself up – it's about learning. This self-reflection is golden, and it helps you steer clear of making the same oopsies again.

Building Resilience: Resilience is like a muscle; the more you work it, the stronger it gets. Remember, everyone trips up sometimes. The trick is to pick yourself up, dust off, and keep your eyes on the prize. Cut yourself some slack, accept that hiccups are part of the journey, and keep pushing forward.

Learning from the Letdowns: There's a lesson in every letdown. Even when things don't pan out, there's always something valuable to take away. Think about what skills you've picked up, even if things didn't turn out how you hoped. These insights could be the key to your next big win.

Rally Your Cheer Squad: Having people with your back makes all the difference. Surround yourself with folks who lift you up and push you forward. Friends, family, mentors – anyone who can share their own stories of bouncing back and give you that extra push when you need it.

Setting Fresh Goals: After a stumble, it's time to set new targets. Use what you've learned to map out your next moves. Break these goals down into smaller steps you can tackle one at a time. This way, you're turning your setback into a setup for future wins.

To Wrap It Up: Failures? Nah, they're steppingstones. With the right mindset, self-reflection, resilience, learning from missteps, a solid support system, and new goals, you're all set to bounce back stronger. Always remember, it's in the face of challenges that we discover what we're made of and build our path to lasting success.

TAKING CONTROL OF YOUR MINDSET: A PATHWAY TO SUCCESS AND PERSONAL GROWTH

In today's ever-changing world, it's easy to feel like we're along for the ride. But here's the thing: we've got way more control than we think, especially regarding our mindset. By taking the reins of our thoughts and actions, we can steer our lives toward success and personal growth. Let's break down how focusing on what's in our control, setting clear goals, and being proactive can change the game.

Zone in on What's in Your Hands: Life sure knows how to throw a wrench in our plans, but there's always something we've got a grip on: our attitude and mindset. Think about it. You get to choose how you react to life's twists and turns. Instead of getting hung up on the stuff you can't change, why not pour your energy into what you can? Look closely at what you're great at, your core values, and all the amazing stuff you bring to the table. That's your gold mine right there. Work on those areas, 'cause they're your ticket to making waves.

Get Clear on Your Goals: Ever feel like you're walking in circles? That's probably because your goals aren't crystal clear. Setting solid, realistic goals is like drawing your own map to Treasure Island. Picture where you wanna be, what you're aiming for. Make your goals

SMART: Specific, Measurable, Achievable, Relevant, and Time-bound. Break 'em down into smaller chunks that you can tackle step by step. Keep these goals in sight, check in on them, and tweak them if you need to. With a clear destination, you're way more likely to hit the bullseye.

Make Your Move: Having a growth mindset isn't just a cool phrase; it's about actually getting up and doing something about your dreams. Shake things up, step outside what's comfy. Look for experiences that challenge you and make you think, "Wow, I did that?" Roll with folks who lift you up and push you to be your best. And when you trip up, don't sweat it. Every misstep is a lesson in disguise. What matters is that you're moving, bit by bit, every single day. It's those small, steady steps that build up to big leaps.

Wrapping It Up: Taking control of your mindset isn't just a choice, it's a must-do if you wanna navigate life like a pro. Sure, we can't dictate everything that happens to us, but our reactions? That's all us. By homing in on what we can control, setting clear goals, and acting, we empower ourselves to shape our journey. Remember, success and growth aren't just endpoints; they're the road we travel every day. Start now, embrace your inner power, and watch as you transform your life, one thought, and one step at a time.

~

SECTION ELEVEN WRAP-UP:

HARNESSING the Power of a Positive Mindset

• **Resilience Factor:** A positive mindset fosters resilience, viewing challenges as opportunities for growth.

• **Learning from the Lows:** Use setbacks as learning experiences, transforming mistakes into growth opportunities.

• **Gratitude and Appreciation:** Practice gratitude to enhance well-being and maintain a positive outlook.

• **Attracting Good Vibes:** A positive attitude attracts opportunities and encourages risk-taking.

• **Mind and Body Wellness:** A positive mindset contributes to better mental and physical health.

Turning Negative Thoughts into Positive Vibes

• **Mindful Moments:** Be aware of negative thoughts and consciously replace them with positive ones.

• **Challenge the Negative:** Analyze and question negative thoughts, replacing them with more logical and positive alternatives.

• **Reframe the Game:** Change negative perspectives into positive ones.

• **Positive Pep-Talk:** Use affirmations to boost self-esteem and maintain a positive outlook.

• **Surround Yourself with Sunshine:** Choose positive influences in your life, including friends, media, and environments.

• **Gratitude Attitude:** Regularly express gratitude to shift focus from negative to positive aspects of life.

• **Lean on Your Squad:** Reach out for support when facing challenges.

• **Self-Care Rituals:** Prioritize self-care activities to foster positive thinking.

Building Your Resilience

• **Life's Hurdles:** View setbacks as opportunities for growth and learning.

• **Stay Positive, Stay Strong:** Maintain a positive attitude, focusing on constructive outcomes and gratitude.

• **Your Squad Matters:** Rely on a supportive network for encouragement and guidance.

• **Keep Calm and Carry On:** Practice stress management techniques like mindfulness and exercise.

• **Problem-Solving Like a Boss:** Focus on solutions rather than dwelling on problems.

• **Self-Care Isn't Selfish:** Prioritize personal well-being to support resilience.

Soaking Up the Good Vibes

• **Friends Who Are Like Sunshine:** Cultivate friendships that are supportive and uplifting.

• **Mentors: Your Personal Life Coaches:** Seek mentorship for guidance and wisdom.

• **Fill Your Feed with Feel-Good:** Consume positive and inspiring content.

Practicing Gratitude and Mindfulness

• **Perks of Gratitude:** Recognize the benefits of gratitude for emotional well-being.

• **Perks of Mindfulness:** Understand how mindfulness can reduce stress and improve focus.

• **Practical Practices:** Incorporate gratitude journals, mindful breathing, and self-care rituals into daily life.

Embracing Failure: The Path to Growth and Strength

• **Growth Mindset:** Adopt a growth mindset to learn from failures and setbacks.

• **Reflect and Analyze:** Use failures as opportunities for introspection and improvement.

• **Building Resilience:** Develop resilience by overcoming challenges and learning from mistakes.

• **Setting Fresh Goals:** Use setbacks as motivation for setting new, achievable goals.

Taking Control of Your Mindset

• **Zone in on What's in Your Hands:** Focus on areas you can control, like your attitude and responses.

• **Get Clear on Your Goals:** Set specific, measurable, and achievable goals.

• **Make Your Move:** Take proactive steps toward personal and professional growth.

ACTION ITEMS:

Harnessing a Positive Mindset

• **Practice Resilience:** When faced with a challenge, look for learning opportunities.

• **Reflect on Setbacks:** Write down lessons learned from recent challenges.

• **Daily Gratitude:** Keep a gratitude journal and note down three things you're thankful for each day.

Turning Negative Thoughts into Positivity

• **Mindfulness Exercise:** Spend 5 minutes each day focusing on your thoughts and gently guiding them toward positivity.

• **Challenge Negativity:** Identify a recurring negative thought and consciously reframe it into something positive.

• **Positive Affirmations:** Create a list of positive affirmations and repeat them daily.

Building Resilience

• **Identify Support Network:** Make a list of people you can rely on during tough times.

• **Stress-Management Techniques:** Incorporate mindfulness or meditation into your routine.

• **Problem-Solving Practice:** Break down a current problem into smaller, manageable tasks.

Soaking Up Good Vibes

• **Cultivate Positive Relationships:** Reach out to a friend who uplifts you and plan a meet-up.

• **Seek a Mentor:** Identify someone you admire and ask for a mentorship session.

• **Positive Media Consumption:** Choose a book or podcast that inspires positivity and spend time with it each week.

Practicing Gratitude and Mindfulness

• **Start a Gratitude Journal:** Write down three things you're grateful for each day.

• **Mindful Breathing:** Allocate time for daily mindful breathing exercises.

• **Mindful Eating:** Practice mindfulness during one meal each day, focusing on the experience.

Embracing Failure as Growth

• **Reflect on a Recent Failure:** Write down what you learned from

In Our Next Section:

In our next section, we'll explore the transformative power of self-reflection and continuous learning. This journey is all about turning the mirror inward and embracing the lifelong quest for knowledge and growth. It's time to dig into how self-reflection not only deepens our understanding of ourselves but also enhances our interactions with the world. We'll unpack strategies to cultivate a habit of introspection, enabling you to identify your values, beliefs, and the driving forces behind your actions. This self-awareness is a cornerstone for personal and professional development, opening doors to a more fulfilling and purposeful life.

Additionally, we'll dive into the world of continuous learning, an important ingredient for staying relevant and invigorated in today's fast-paced environment. You'll discover how to keep your intellectual curiosity alive and kicking, turning every experience, whether a success or setback, into a learning opportunity. We'll explore methods to maintain an ever-evolving skill set, ensuring you remain adaptable and resilient in the face of change. This section aims to inspire and equip you with the tools to see every day as a chance to grow, learn, and edge closer to your best self. Prepare to start a journey of self-discovery and relentless learning, where the only constant is your commitment to personal evolution.

~

SECTION TWELVE: CULTIVATING EMOTIONAL INTELLIGENCE FOR EFFECTIVE COMMUNICATION DURING DIFFICULT SITUATIONS

UNDERSTANDING EMOTIONAL INTELLIGENCE:

EMOTIONAL INTELLIGENCE, or EQ, is like having a superpower for dealing with our own feelings and those of others. It's all about getting the hang of recognizing, understanding, and handling emotions in a way that's positive and effective. EQ is a big deal when it comes to talking through tough stuff, because it can help us keep our cool, connect better, and come up with solutions that work for everyone.

When we're in the thick of a tricky chat, emotions can get intense, and it's easy to slip into reactions that don't help. That's where EQ comes in. It helps us stay chill and empathetic, which is key to getting our points across without making a mess of things. Getting what's going on emotionally – both with ourselves and others – is a game-changer for responding in ways that build understanding and a real emotional bond.

Here are the four biggies of EQ:

1. Self-awareness: This is all about tuning into your own emotions, strengths, and not-so-strong points. It's knowing what sets you off and how your feelings sway your thoughts and actions. Self-awareness is useful in tough conversations because it helps you figure out where you're coming from and respond thoughtfully instead of reacting.

2. Self-management: This one's about steering your emotions in a helpful direction, even when the pressure's on. It's like being the captain of your emotional ship, keeping things steady through the storm. Managing your feelings means you can keep your cool and think clearly, which is important when you're hashing things out.

3. Social awareness: Ever wish you could read minds? Social awareness is the next best thing. It's picking up on what others are feeling and needing, even if they don't spell it out. This skill is key for creating a space where everyone feels understood and valued, which can make a world of difference in a tough conversation.

4. Relationship management: This is about building and keeping strong, healthy connections with others. It involves being a top-notch communicator, sorting out conflicts in a positive way, and affecting others that's good for everyone. This part of EQ helps you find common ground, tackle issues without burning bridges, and keep relationships solid and respectful.

Briefly, EQ is your best buddy for navigating the choppy waters of difficult discussions. It's about knowing yourself, handling your emotions, getting the emotional vibe of others, and maintaining relationships that rock. With a strong EQ, you're all set to communicate like a pro, solve problems together, and build connections that last.

RECOGNIZING EMOTIONS:

EMOTIONAL SMARTS – that's what recognizing our own emotions and those of the people around us is all about. It's a biggie in emotional intelligence and is all about making sense of what we're feeling, why we're feeling it, and how others are feeling, too. Getting good at this can be a game-changer for your personal relationships, decision-making, and even your mental health. Let's look at some solid ways to get better at figuring out all those feels:

Mindfulness: It's like giving your mind a workout. Practicing mindfulness means tuning into your thoughts, feelings, and body signals without any kind of judgment. You could try meditating, or take a few minutes each day to check in with yourself. This way, you get a clearer picture of your emotions and can understand others' feelings better too.

Journaling: Grab a pen and let it all out on paper. Writing about your day, how you felt, and why you think you felt that way can help you spot emotional patterns and triggers. It's like being your own detective, but for emotions!

Reflecting on the Past: Think back to times you felt emotional. What set you off? How did you react? Reflecting on these moments, maybe with a friend or a therapist, can give you new insights and help you manage similar situations better.

Feedback Time: Sometimes, we need an outside view. Ask people you trust for honest feedback about how you come across. It's like holding up a mirror to your emotional world – sometimes you see stuff you've missed.

Active Listening: When you're talking to someone, listen. Don't just hear their words; pay attention to how they say them, their body language, everything. This deep listening builds empathy and helps you get the emotional undercurrents in conversations.

Walk in Their Shoes: Empathy is key. Try to understand how others might feel by putting yourself in their shoes. Ask questions, be curious, and genuinely care about their answers. It's all about connecting on a deeper emotional level.

Manage Those Emotions: We all get emotional, but the trick is handling those emotions in a healthy way. Learn to chill out with techniques like deep breathing or taking a quick walk. This helps you react to your feelings in a calm, collected way and be more considerate of others' feelings too.

So, there you have it – a roadmap to emotional wisdom. Practice these steps regularly, and you'll be amazed at how much more in tune you'll be with your own emotions and the emotions of those around you. It's all about building stronger connections, making smarter decisions, and leading a happier, more balanced life.

MANAGING EMOTIONS:

ALL RIGHT LET's talk about keeping cool under pressure. When things get tough, our emotions can go haywire, but there are solid ways to keep them in check. Here's a rundown of strategies to stay level-headed:

Deep Breathing: This is a classic for a reason. When you feel those emotions bubbling up, take a moment for some deep breaths. Breathe in slowly through your nose, hold it for a sec, and then let it out through your mouth. Do this a few times and you'll notice a big difference. It's like hitting the reset button on your stress.

Hit Pause: In a sticky situation, give yourself a time-out. Before you react, just pause. This gives you a chance to step back, cool off, and get a better view of things. It's like stepping out of the emotional whirlwind so you can think more clearly.

Know Yourself: Being clued into what sets you off is huge. Pay attention to your triggers and how you typically react. Are those reactions helping or hurting the situation? The more you know about your emotional habits, the better you can handle them.

Mindfulness: This one's all about living in the now. Whether it's meditation, yoga, or being totally in the moment with whatever you're doing, mindfulness helps you get a grip on your emotions by not letting your mind wander into stress-land.

Lean on Your Crew: When things are rough, don't go it alone. Chat with friends, family, or even a pro if you need to. Sometimes talking it out can give you a fresh perspective or the relief you need.

Rethink It: This is about tweaking your thought patterns. If you catch yourself going down a negative thought spiral, try to flip the script. Replace those not-so-helpful thoughts with ones that are more positive and realistic.

Relaxation Techniques: Figure out what chills you out. Maybe it's painting, going for a run, listening to your favorite tunes, or chilling in nature. Find your happy place activities and make time for them, especially when the stress dial turns up.

Remember, getting a handle on your emotions isn't a one-size-fits-all thing, and it's definitely not an overnight fix. It's about trying different things, seeing what clicks for you, and being kind to yourself while you figure it out. Keep at it, and you'll find your groove in managing those tricky emotional moments.

EMPATHY AND PERSPECTIVE-TAKING:

EMPATHY AND PERSPECTIVE-TAKING are like superpowers regarding emotional intelligence, especially in tricky conversations or problem-solving. Here's the lowdown on why they're so key:

Empathy: This is all about getting what someone else is feeling. It's like putting yourself in their shoes and tuning into their emotions. When you show empathy, you're not just understanding their feelings, but you're also letting them know they're heard and that their feelings matter. This builds trust and openness in communication, which is helpful when things get tough.

Perspective-Taking: Think of this as looking at a situation through someone else's goggles. It's about understanding where they're coming from, even if it's different from your view. This skill is a game-changer for working out problems because it brings in many view-points and ideas you might not have thought of. It helps cut through biases and gets you thinking more clearly and fairly.

So, why are these skills so awesome?

Better Connections: When you empathize with folks, you're building stronger, deeper relationships. It's easier to chat and get things done when everyone feels respected and understood.

Creative Problem-Solving: If there's a disagreement or a tough problem, understanding different sides can lead to some clever solutions that work for everyone. You get more ideas on the table and find solutions that might have been missed otherwise.

Improved Communication: Seeing things from another angle helps you talk about your own thoughts and feelings without getting all defensive or aggressive. It's about chatting in a way that's respectful and kind.

Boosted Emotional Intelligence: Empathy and perspective-taking are big parts of emotional intelligence, which includes knowing your own emotions, managing them, and being motivated. This whole package is important for getting along with others, managing sticky situations, and succeeding both personally and professionally.

To sum it up, empathy and perspective-taking are like your secret weapons for better communication, smarter problem-solving, and building real connections. They help you get where others are coming from, which makes life smoother and more harmonious all around.

ACTIVE LISTENING AND NONVERBAL COMMUNICATION:

Active listening and nonverbal communication are like the dynamic duo of emotional intelligence. They're important in understanding and managing emotions – both yours and others. These skills are the secret sauce for successful relationships, whether you're at work or chilling with friends. They help you communicate like a pro, build trust, and show you get what others are feeling.

Active Listening: Here's the deal with active listening – it's all about tuning in to what the other person is saying. It's not just waiting for your turn to speak. It's about genuinely hearing them out. Techniques like paraphrasing or summarizing are brilliant for this. When you paraphrase, you're basically repeating what the person said, but in your own words. It's like saying, "Hey, I hear you, and this is what I understand." Summarizing is like hitting the highlights – giving a quick recap of the key points. Both these techniques make sure you're on the same page and show the speaker they're being heard.

Nonverbal Communication: Body language and facial expressions are huge in communication. Did you know that some experts say they make up 70-80% of all communication? That's massive! Things like gestures, eye contact, how you stand or sit, and the expressions on your face speak volumes. For example, if someone's got their arms crossed and a frown on, they might feel defensive or uncomfortable, even if they're saying everything's fine. So, paying attention to these cues is essential. It helps you catch what's not being said out loud. And don't forget about your own nonverbal signals. They can show others you're engaged and empathetic.

Briefly: Active listening and nonverbal communication are key to beefing up your emotional intelligence. Using strategies like para-phrasing and summarizing makes conversations more meaningful. Plus, being clued into body language and facial expressions lets you pick up on those unspoken vibes. By getting good at these skills, you'll be better at connecting with people, earning their trust, and showing empathy. And that's a win-win in anyone's book!

CONFLICT RESOLUTION SKILLS:

Navigating conflicts and sorting out disagreements is important, both in our personal lives and at work. Using emotional intelligence can go a long way in these situations. It's all about empathy, knowing yourself, and communicating in a way that gets to the heart of the issue. Let's break down cool strategies to make this happen:

Know Yourself First: Before jumping into any conflict resolution, it's a good idea to check in with yourself. What's setting you off? What emotions are you feeling? Getting a handle on your own reactions helps you keep your cool and stay clear-headed during the discussion.

Empathetic Listening: Listen like a pro. I mean, listen to what the other person is saying. Try to see where they're coming from and acknowledge their feelings. It's not about getting ready to fire back with your side; it's about understanding theirs.

Finding Common Ground: There's usually something you agree on or a shared goal you can focus on. Finding that common ground can be a great way to start working together instead of against each other. It's all about finding a spot where everyone's more chill and ready to compromise.

Stay Cool: Keeping your cool is key. Getting all hot-headed or emotional often just makes things worse. Practice keeping calm – maybe take deep breaths, pause before answering, and keep your voice steady. It sets the tone for a more constructive chat.

Use "I" Statements: It's like saying, "I feel this way when…" instead of "You always do this…" It helps to share your side without making the other person feel like they're being attacked. It's a smoother way to get your point across.

Aim for a Win-Win: You're not in a boxing match. The goal is to find a solution that works for everyone. Brainstorm together and try to come up with ideas that tackle the real issues and make both sides happy.

Take a Time-Out if Needed: If things get too heated, it's okay to hit the pause button. Taking a break lets everyone cool off and think things through. Then, you can come back with a clearer head.

Get a Mediator: When things are tough, it might be a good idea to bring in someone neutral. A mediator can help keep things on track and make sure everyone's being heard.

So, remember, conflict's just part of life. Handling it with emotional smarts can actually make your relationships stronger and lead to some solid solutions. By using these strategies, you're setting yourself up for a more peaceful and productive outcome.

PRACTICE AND APPLICATION:

Congratulations on completing the chapter on emotional intelligence! Now that you have learned about the importance of emotional intelligence and its impact on communication, it's time to put your knowledge into action. Here are a few exercises, role-playing scenarios, and real-life examples to help you practice and apply emotional intelligence skills to difficult communication situations:

Exercise: Self-awareness Journal

Take out a journal or a notebook and set aside some time each day to reflect on your emotions and reactions. Write down situations where you felt strong emotions, whether positive or negative. Identify the triggers, your initial emotional response, and how you handled the situation. This exercise will help you learn your emotions and let you start managing them effectively.

Role-playing Scenario: Resolving a Conflict

Enlist the help of a friend, family member, or colleague to role-play a conflict situation. This could be an argument, a disagreement, or a difficult conversation. Practice using active listening skills, empathetic responses, and nonverbal cues to understand the other person's perspective and defuse tension. Focus on regulating your emotions and finding a mutually beneficial solution to the conflict.

Real-life Example: Providing Feedback

Think of a recent situation where you had to give feedback to someone. It could be a coworker, a friend, or a family member. Reflect on how you approached the conversation and whether you effectively communicated your thoughts and feelings. Consider the impact of your words and body language and assess whether your feedback was well-received and constructive. If there is room for improvement, brainstorm alternative approaches that align with emotional intelligence principles.

Exercise: Mindful Listening

Choose a conversation partner, preferably someone whose perspective or experiences differ from yours. Engage in a conversation where you actively practice mindful listening. This means putting aside your own judgments and preconceptions, genuinely focusing on the other person's words, emotions, and nonverbal cues. Try to empathize and understand their perspective before responding. Reflect on the impact this has on the quality of conversation and your ability to connect with others.

Role-playing Scenario: Delivering Bad News

Role-play a scenario where you have to deliver bad news to someone. This could inform a colleague of a project delay, letting a friend know about a personal setback, or discussing a difficult topic with a family member. Practice using empathy to convey your understanding of their feelings, active listening to confirm their emotions, and clear, concise communication to deliver the news sensitively. Aim to find a balance between being compassionate and providing necessary information.

By engaging in these exercises, role-playing scenarios, and real-life examples, you will actively apply the ideas and techniques learned in the chapter on emotional intelligence. Remember, practice is key to developing your emotional intelligence skills and becoming a better communicator. The more you practice, the more natural these skills will become, and the more effectively you will navigate difficult communication situations. Good luck!

SECTION TWELVE WRAP-UP:

UNDERSTANDING EMOTIONAL INTELLIGENCE:

- Emotional intelligence (EQ) helps manage feelings positively and effectively.
- EQ components: Self-awareness, self-management, social awareness, relationship management.

Recognizing Emotions:

- Essential for understanding both our feelings and others'.
- Techniques: Mindfulness, journaling, reflecting on past emotions, seeking feedback, active listening, empathy, managing emotions.

Managing Emotions:

- Strategies for staying calm under pressure.

- Includes deep breathing, taking a pause, knowing triggers, practicing mindfulness, seeking support, reframing thoughts, relaxation techniques.

Empathy and Perspective-Taking:

- Key for understanding and communicating effectively in difficult situations.
- Benefits: Better connections, creative problem-solving, improved communication, boosted EQ.

Active Listening and Nonverbal Communication:

- Essential for understanding underlying emotions and meanings in conversations.
- Involves techniques like paraphrasing, summarizing, and being aware of body language.

Conflict Resolution Skills:

- Vital for resolving disagreements positively.
- Strategies include self-awareness, empathetic listening, finding common ground, staying calm, using "I" statements, aiming for win-win solutions, taking breaks, and involving mediators.

ACTION ITEMS:

Practice Self-awareness:

- Regularly reflect on your emotions and responses to improve understanding and management of feelings.

Mindfulness Meditation:

- Incorporate mindfulness practices like meditation or yoga to enhance emotional regulation and awareness.

Journaling for Emotional Clarity:

- Keep a journal to track and understand your emotional triggers and patterns.

Seek Constructive Feedback:

- Ask for feedback from trusted individuals to gain perspective on your emotional expressions and communication style.

Engage in Active Listening:

- Practice deep listening in conversations to build empathy and understanding.

Empathy Exercises:

- Put yourself in others' shoes in various situations to develop empathy and perspective-taking skills.

Learn Relaxation Techniques:

- Use relaxation methods like deep breathing, mindfulness, or hobbies to manage stress and emotions.

Conflict Resolution Role-Playing:

- Engage in role-playing exercises to practice and improve your conflict resolution skills.

Emotional Regulation Practice:

- In challenging situations, consciously practice emotional regulation techniques to maintain calmness.

Regular Self-Reflection:

- Dedicate time for self-reflection to continually develop your emotional intelligence and communication skills.

In Our Next Section:

In our next section, we'll dive into the art of effective decision-making under pressure. Life's full of moments where you've got to make choices – sometimes in a snap. How you handle these decisions can shape your path, both in your career and personal life. This section is all about mastering the skills to make wise, timely decisions, even when the heat is on. We'll explore techniques to stay clear-headed, weigh your options smartly, and trust your gut. It's about turning pressure into your ally, transforming tough choices into steppingstones for success.

We'll also tackle the importance of strategic planning in uncertain times. Life's unpredictable, but that doesn't mean you can't have a game plan. Whether it's your career goals, personal projects, or unexpected challenges, having a strategy helps you navigate through the fog. It's like having a map in the wilderness – you might not know every twist and turn ahead, but you'll have a direction to move in. This section will equip you with the tools to craft flexible, effective strategies, making sure you stay on track toward your goals, no matter what life throws your way. Let's get ready to become masters of decision-making and strategic planning!

SECTION THIRTEEN: BALANCING WORK AND LIFE WHEN DEALING WITH UNEXPECTED CHALLENGES

NAVIGATING UNEXPECTED CHALLENGES IN PERSONAL AND PROFESSIONAL LIFE

LIFE RARELY GOES ACCORDING to plan, as unexpected challenges have a way of throwing us off balance. Whether it's a health issue, a family emergency, or any other unforeseen circumstance, being prepared and knowing how to recognize these challenges is important. By gaining awareness about the types of unexpected challenges that can arise, individuals can develop resilience and create strategies to overcome them. Here's a rundown on some common unexpected challenges and how to skate through them like a pro:

Health Hiccups: Your health's a big deal, but sometimes it throws a wrench in the works. Whether it's a sudden flu, a long-term illness, or feeling rundown, it's key to listen to your body. Look out for burnout or stress signs, and don't shy away from getting help when you need it. Staying on top of your fitness game, eating right, and getting enough shut-eye can be real game-changers here.

Family Emergencies: Family stuff can come out of left field – like needing to care for someone sick or dealing with a sudden loss. The best bet? Keep the lines of communication open at home. Have a plan for when things go sideways and know your limits. Balancing family needs and work can be tough, but setting clear boundaries helps.

Money Matters: Ah, money – it has a way of making things interesting, especially with surprise expenses or job changes. Having a rainy-day fund and a solid budget plan is smart. If things get tight, financial advice or side gigs could help keep you afloat.

Workplace Wobbles: Work isn't always smooth sailing. You might face team spats, big company shake-ups, or even job loss. Stay alert to signs of stress and burnout. Having a solid network, versatile skills, and keeping up with what's hot in your industry can help you steer through these choppy waters.

Tech Troubles: In our digital world, tech troubles like hacks or system crashes can throw a spanner in the works. Stay sharp on cybersecurity, back up your important stuff, and have a plan for tech hiccups, both at work and at home.

In a Nutshell: Life's rollercoaster can take you on some wild rides. But with a little prep and resilience, you can ride out those unexpected challenges. Stay healthy, build strong connections, and always have a plan B. Remember, tough times don't last, but tough people do. Keep your chin up, tackle each problem head-on, and you'll grow stronger and wiser.

~

EVALUATING PRIORITIES:

When life tosses you a wobble, it's time to take a good hard look at what's on your plate and shuffle things around. Balancing your workload and personal life is key, especially when unexpected stuff pops up. Here's a guide on how to juggle your priorities like a pro:

Time for Some Soul-Searching: Hit the pause button and think about what matters to you, both at work and outside of it. Ask yourself: "What's my big picture here?" This bit of self-reflection is your compass for making smart choices.

Weighing the Impact: Look at how this new twist affects your to-do list. Is it a five-alarm fire, or can it chill on the back burner? Figure out what needs your attention right now and what the long game looks like.

Chit-Chat and Teamwork: If this curveball affects others, get talking. Share what's up, brainstorm together, and divvy up the tasks. Good communication can ease the pressure and get everyone pulling in the same direction.

Prioritize and Pass the Baton: Spot the must-dos and figure out what you can hand off to someone else. Focus on the stuff that feeds into your bigger goals, and don't be shy about delegating the rest.

Carve Out Your Time: Use time blocking to create a schedule that balances work stuff, personal time, and those all-important chill moments. This way, you've got a plan for tackling everything that matters.

Draw the Line and Learn to Say Nope: Be firm about your limits and turn down stuff that doesn't fit with your main goals. It's okay to say no – it keeps you from spreading yourself too thin.

Keep Checking In: Life's always changing, and so are your priorities. Make a habit of reassessing what's on your plate to make sure it still lines up with your goals and what's important to you.

Go Easy on Yourself: Lastly, cut yourself some slack. Not everything's under your control, and that's okay. Be flexible with your plans and don't beat yourself up when things go sideways.

Remember, getting your priorities straight isn't a one-time deal – it's an ongoing process. By staying mindful of what you need to focus on, you can ride out life's little surprises without dropping the ball on what's key.

SETTING BOUNDARIES:

DRAWING the line between your work and personal life is key for keeping things chill and avoiding total burnout. We all know how nuts it can get with work stuff spilling over into our downtime. So, here's the deal on setting those boundaries to keep your cool:

1. Time for You: You gotta carve out time for yourself. When you're off the clock, dive into stuff that recharges you – hit the gym, hang with family and friends, get into your hobbies, or just kick back and relax. If you're always in work mode, you'll end up fried and creativity takes a nosedive.

2. Keep Your Relationships Rockin': Your peeps – family, pals – they're your rock. Keeping work separate means, you can be there for them, and they for you. It's all about making those moments count without work looming over your head. Don't let your job nudge out the folks who matter most.

3. Strike That Balance: It's like juggling. You want to ace it at work and in your personal life without dropping the ball. Setting clear lines helps you focus where and when it counts. It's about being all in at work during work hours and switching off when it's time for life stuff. This way, you're more dialed-in and efficient in both worlds.

4. Communicate Your Limits: Let the people at work know your boundaries. Set your work hours and stick to them. Make it clear when you're off the grid for work calls and emails. It's all about setting expectations so everyone's on the same page.

5. Smart Time Management: Get your priorities straight. Figure out what needs your attention most, both at work and at home. Scheduling, focusing on the big stuff, and delegating when you can are all part of the mix. It helps you give your best where it's needed most.

Remember, setting these boundaries isn't just good for you; it amps up your game at work and makes life outside the office way more awesome. By focusing on your well-being, you're not just happier – you're more productive and creative too. So go ahead, draw those lines and enjoy the best of both worlds!

SEEKING SUPPORT:

Let's talk about why it's important to seek support when the going gets tough, whether it's in our personal lives or on the job.

Kicking Loneliness to the Curb: Sometimes life hits us hard with stuff like relationship woes, health scares, or losing someone close. It's during these tough times that contacting our buddies, family, or even a support group can make a difference. Talking it out with someone can help you feel like you're not in this alone. The comfort and understanding you get from your inner circle are huge for keeping your head above water emotionally.

Workplace Backup: At work, things can get tricky too, what with crazy deadlines, office drama, or career crossroads. This is when tapping into the wisdom of your work pals, mentors, or your professional network can be a game-changer. Your coworkers might have nifty tips or could lend a hand with complex tasks. Mentors are great for wisdom and advice, and your professional network can hook you up with resources, fresh ideas, and maybe even new opportunities.

Fresh Perspectives: Sharing your challenges with others opens up new ways of looking at things. You might just stumble upon solutions or ideas you hadn't thought of before. Getting a different point of view can be a real eye-opener and can help you tackle problems from a new angle.

Learning from the Pros: There's nothing like learning from people who've been in your shoes. Chatting with folks who've faced similar challenges can give you some solid advice and save you from making the same mistakes they did. You can pick up some smart strategies and feel more prepared to handle what's coming.

Finding Your Tribe: Connecting with people who get what you're going through creates a sense of community and belonging. It's comforting to know you're not the only one dealing with certain issues. Being part of a group that supports each other can boost your morale and keep you motivated.

Reaching out for support when life gets bumpy is important for both your personal life and career. It helps you feel less alone, gives you new viewpoints, lets you learn from others, and builds a sense of community. So next time you're facing a tough spot, don't hesitate to lean on those around you. Together, you're stronger and can tackle anything!

DEVELOPING RESILIENCE:

HEY THERE! Building resilience is like kitting out your toolkit for life's surprises. It's about staying strong, no matter what comes your way, without letting your work-life balance topple over. Let's dive into some key strategies to beef up that resilience:

1. Positive Mindset Magic:

• **Gratitude Galore:** Take time to count your blessings, both at work and home. It shifts your focus to the good stuff.

• **Pep Talk:** Swap out those downer thoughts with some upbeat self-chatter. Remember your wins and strengths, and keep your eyes on what you can actually change.

• **Change Champion:** Instead of fighting change, greet it with open arms. Look at challenges as chances to learn and grow.

2. Self-Care is Key:

• **Snooze to Win:** Prioritize your zzz's for both your body and brain's sake. And hey, don't forget to take little breaks to recharge your batteries.

• **Eat Smart:** Fuel up with food good for both body and mind. It's like giving your resilience a power-up.

• **Move It:** Regular exercise isn't just good for your health; it's a stress-buster and mood-lifter, perfect for resilience building.

3. Emotional Well-being Toolbox:

• **Master Your Emotions:** Work on ways to handle your feelings in a healthy way. This could be through calming breathing, staying in the moment, or jotting down your thoughts.

• **Your Support Squad:** Stay connected with friends, family, or coworkers who get you. Do stuff that strengthens these bonds.

• **Flexibility & Adaptability:** Learn to roll with the punches. Stay open to new ways of doing things and switching up plans when needed.

4. Time Management & Boundary Setting:

• **What Matters Most:** Figure out your top tasks and focus your energy there. Aim for results over busy work.

• **Delegate to Elevate:** Trust others to take the wheel sometimes. It eases your load and keeps things moving smoothly.

• **Draw the Line:** Be clear about your limits with everyone. This means setting work hours and personal time firmly.

5. Learning and Reflecting:

• **Look Back to Leap Forward:** Think about times you've rocked a tough situation. What worked? Use those tactics again.

• **Failures Are Lessons:** Flip your failures into learning opportunities. Each misstep has something to teach.

• **Never Stop Learning:** Keep boosting your skills and knowledge. It ups your confidence and your game in handling new challenges.

6. Break Time & Disconnect:

• **Take Five (or Fifteen):** Regular breaks during your day can recharge you big time. Unplug from work stuff and just chill.

• **Vacation Mode:** Plan proper time off to relax and step away from work. Use this time to dive into hobbies or activities you love.

Building resilience isn't an overnight thing – it's a day-by-day journey. By weaving these strategies into your everyday life, you'll be better equipped to handle whatever life throws at you while keeping your work and personal life in a sweet balance.

CREATING A FLEXIBLE SCHEDULE:

CRAFTING a schedule that bends but doesn't break under surprise pressures is essential. It's all about balancing the unexpected with your work and chill time. Let's jump into some tips to make a schedule that's as flexible as a yoga master:

1. **Work with Wiggle Room:**

   - **Chat about Flex Work:** See if you can tweak your work hours or work from home when life throws a wrench in your plans. This bit of leeway can be a lifesaver for those out-of-the-blue appointments or family stuff.
   - **Set Your Time Zone:** Make it known when you're on the clock and when you're off. This way, your team and your family know when you're in work mode and when you're in me-time mode.

2. **Tackle Tasks Like a Pro:**

   - **List and Prioritize:** Whip up a to-do list and rank tasks by their "gotta do it now" level. This keeps you zeroed in on what's top priority.

- **Block It Like It's Hot:** Carve out chunks of your day for different tasks – like meetings, solo work, or breaks. This setup helps you manage your day without getting tangled in too many things at once.

3. **Keep Everyone in the Loop:**

- **Clear as Crystal Communication:** Keep your colleagues and clients in the loop about your schedule and any tweaks you make. It's all about setting the right expectations.
- **Helping Hands:** Don't shy away from delegating or asking for a hand. Sharing the load can lighten your stress and open up space for those curveballs.

4. **Self-Care isn't Selfish:**

- **Make Time for You:** Block out times for exercise, hobbies, or hanging with loved ones. A relaxed and recharged you is better at tackling problems head-on.
- **Flexibility is Key:** Accept that plans will need to change sometimes. Be cool with shifting things around and rejigging your to-dos.

5. **Reflect and Grow:**

- **Review and Learn:** After you've dealt with a surprise challenge, take a sec to think about how it went down. What worked? What didn't? Learning from these moments helps you handle the next one even better.

Flexibility and adaptability aren't overnight things; they're skills you improve at over time. By weaving these tips into your daily life, you'll craft a schedule ready for whatever, while keeping your work and life in a happy harmony.

SECTION THIRTEEN WRAP-UP:

KEY POINTS:

IMPORTANCE OF WORK-LIFE BALANCE: Maintaining a balance between professional and personal life is important for overall well-being, including mental and physical health, and ensuring productive and creative work output.

- **Navigating Unexpected Challenges:** Be ready to face unpredictable situations in both personal and professional life, such as health issues, family emergencies, and workplace changes, and develop resilience to overcome them.
- **Evaluating Priorities:** Regularly assess what's important in both personal and work life, especially when facing unexpected challenges, to maintain focus and effectiveness.
- **Setting Boundaries:** Clearly define the separation between work and personal time to prevent burnout and to ensure time for self and relationships.
- **Seeking Support:** Don't hesitate to reach out for help in both personal and professional spheres during challenging times for advice, perspectives, and emotional support.

- **Developing Resilience:** Cultivate a positive mindset, practice self-care, manage emotions effectively, and learn from experiences to build resilience.
- **Creating a Flexible Schedule:** Adaptability in scheduling is key to balancing work and personal life, especially when dealing with unforeseen circumstances.

ACTION ITEMS:

- **Self-Care:** Schedule regular activities for physical and mental well-being, such as exercise, hobbies, or relaxation techniques.
- **Communication:** Keep open lines of communication with family and colleagues to manage expectations and seek support during challenging times.
- **Financial Planning:** Establish a budget and savings plan to prepare for unexpected financial needs.
- **Workplace Strategies:** Develop skills to adapt to changes at work, like learning new technologies or staying informed about industry trends.
- **Mindfulness Practices:** Incorporate mindfulness or meditation into daily routines to enhance emotional well-being and stress management.
- **Network Building:** Actively build and maintain a support network of friends, family, mentors, and professional contacts.
- **Goal Setting:** Regularly review and adjust personal and professional goals to align with current priorities and challenges.
- **Boundary Setting:** Clearly define work hours and personal time and communicate these boundaries to colleagues and family.
- **Delegation:** Learn to delegate tasks effectively both at work and home to manage workload and stress.
- **Reflective Practices:** Engage in regular self-reflection and learning from experiences to improve handling of future challenges.

- **Schedule Flexibility:** Plan a flexible daily schedule that allows for changes in case of unexpected events or responsibilities.
- **Review and Adjust:** Continuously assess and adjust strategies for work-life balance based on effectiveness and personal well-being.

In Our Next Section:

In our next section, we'll dig into the transformative journey of personal development. This is about embracing the rollercoaster of life, with all its twists and turns, and coming out stronger and more self-aware. We'll explore the essence of continuous learning and growth, highlighting strategies to evolve, adapt, and thrive in the face of life's ongoing changes. You'll discover how to harness your experiences, both good and bad, as powerful tools for personal enrichment.

Remember, personal development isn't a destination; it's a never-ending journey. It's about setting your sights on becoming the best version of yourself, no matter the circumstances. We'll discuss how to set achievable goals, foster a growth mindset, and cultivate habits that lead to sustained success and fulfillment. This section is designed to be your roadmap, guiding you through the process of self-discovery and empowerment. So, gear up for an insightful journey that promises to equip you with the mindset and skills needed to turn life's challenges into steppingstones for personal triumph.

SECTION FOURTEEN:
SEEKING PROFESSIONAL
HELP AND GUIDANCE

RECOGNIZING THE NEED FOR PROFESSIONAL HELP AND GUIDANCE

REALIZING you need a hand from the pros is a big step toward bettering yourself and your overall happiness. It's brave to say, "Hey, I might need some extra help here." Choosing professional guidance isn't just a smart move; it's a power play for some positive life changes.

So, when should you consider calling in the experts? Here's a rundown:

Mental Health Matters:

- **Feeling Overwhelmed?** Conditions like anxiety, depression, or addiction can mess with your day-to-day life and joy. A therapist or counselor can hook you up with tactics to manage your thoughts and feelings in a healthier way. They've got insights and advice that can flip the script on your mental health game.

Life's Big Hurdles:

- **Tough Times:** Big changes or setbacks—like losing your job, going through a divorce, getting sick, or dealing with loss—can knock the wind out of you. Whether it's getting tips from a career coach, financial advice, or a shoulder to lean on from a grief counselor, professional help can be a lifesaver in getting you back on track.

Personal Growth Goals:

- **Leveling Up:** If you're aiming to kick habits, up your communication game, or hit some career goals, sometimes you need an expert in your corner. Life coaches or career counselors can clear the fog, help you set solid goals, and work out how to leap over any hurdles in your way.

Remember, reaching out for professional help isn't a sign of defeat; it's a sign you're taking charge. It's about valuing yourself enough to say, "I deserve the best shot at a happy, successful life." So, if you're thinking you might not have all the answers, that's okay. By seeking expert guidance, you're actively shaping your life and setting yourself up for some awesome wins.

$\sim$

RESEARCHING AND FINDING RELIABLE PROFESSIONALS

TAPPING into a pro's brainpower can make a difference in many situations. Whether you're trying to crack a tough nut in a particular area or need a hand making big decisions, these experts bring a lot to the table. Here's what you stand to gain by getting them on your side:

They Know Their Stuff:

- **Expert Insight:** These folks have put in the hours and have the smarts in their field. They get the fine details and can tailor their know-how to what you specifically need.

Outside Looking In:

- **Fresh Eyes:** A big plus of going to a pro is they see things from the outside. They can weigh up your situation without any personal hang-ups muddling the view. This can be a game-changer when you're trying to make tough calls.

Smooth Operators:

- **Skill and Speed:** Years in the game mean they've got the moves down pat. They've got tricks, techniques, and tools that make things run like clockwork. This can save you time, hassle, and headaches.

The Right Contacts:

- **Who You Know:** These experts often have a little black book that's worth its weight in gold. They can hook you up with other top minds, open doors to opportunities, or get you access to stuff you can't just Google. This can give you a real edge.

Playing It Safe:

- **Dodging Pitfalls:** Going it alone can be risky, especially if you're out of your depth. Pros can spot the icebergs ahead and help you steer clear. They think about all the what-ifs so you don't end up with regrets.

Level Up:

- **Grow Your Own Know-How:** This isn't just about getting a task done. It's a chance to learn from the best. You'll pick up pointers and get more confident handling similar stuff down the road.

Getting professional expertise is more than just outsourcing a problem. It's about deep insight, fair advice, saving time, making connections, reducing risks, and growing your own skills. Whether it's legal, financial, health, or any other area, these pros can guide you to better decisions and a smoother path forward.

~

TACKLING THE STIGMA OF ASKING FOR HELP: WHY IT'S COOL TO GET A PRO'S PERSPECTIVE

THERE'S this weird hang-up folks have about reaching out for help, especially when it's about mental health. It's like there's this unwritten rule you gotta tough it out on your own, and asking for help is a no-go. But, let's be real – that's just not how it should be. Here's why getting a professional's take can be a game-changer:

Understanding What's Up with Your Head:

- **Pro Insight:** Mental health pros have the smarts to figure out what's cooking in your brain. They can spot what's going on and give you the lowdown on how to tackle it. It's like having a personal detective for your mind.

A Safe Space to Spill:

- **Judgment-Free Zone:** These experts are all about listening with no side-eye. They give you space to lay everything out on the table – fears, dreams, the whole shebang – in a chill environment.

Boosting Your Overall Vibe:

- **Life Upgrade:** If mental health issues are left to brew, they can start messing with everything – your relationships, job, even your body. Getting some help can put you back in the driver's seat, helping you steer toward a happier life.

Top-Notch Tactics:

- **The Right Tools:** These folks have a toolbox of strategies that are proven to work. We're talking therapies and treatments with the science stamp of approval. It's like getting the best gear for your brain.

Ditching the Lone-Wolf Act:

- **Power in Numbers:** Society often bigs up the whole lone-wolf, deal-with-it-alone attitude. But, teaming up with a pro shows there's strength in reaching out. It's about sharing the load, not carrying it all on your own shoulders.

Briefly, kicking the stigma of asking for help to the curb means realizing that getting a pro's help is a strong move. It's about getting clued up on your mental health, having a safe place to talk, boosting your life quality, grabbing the best mental tools, and understanding that it's okay to lean on someone. It's a power play for taking care of you.

NAVIGATING THE MENTAL HEALTH PRO SCENE: PSYCHOLOGISTS, THERAPISTS, COUNSELORS, OH MY!

EVER FELT BAFFLED by all the mental health pros out there? You're not alone. Let's break down the roles of psychologists, therapists, and counselors to make things clearer.

Psychologists:

- **Brainy Bunch:** These folks have a heavyweight title – a PhD or PsyD in psychology. They're the gurus of human behavior and mental gymnastics. Think assessments, tests, and therapy sessions to get folks back on track. Some are also into research or teaching at universities.

Therapists:

- **The Broad Spectrum:** The term 'therapist' covers a bunch of different pros. We're talking about licensed clinical social workers (LCSWs), marriage and family therapists (LMFTs), and professional counselors (LPCs), who usually hold master's degrees. These pros are all about talking therapies – helping individuals, couples, or groups handle mental health hiccups, relationship tangles, and life's curveballs.

Counselors:

- **Focus Experts:** Counselors, much like therapists, work with individuals and groups, but they often specialize in particular areas. Think mental health, schools, addiction, or careers. With master's degrees and licenses in their areas, they guide folks through rough patches, helping set goals and develop skills to tackle challenges head-on.

Choosing Your Mental Health Maverick:

- **Know the Territory:** Keep in mind that what these pros are called can vary depending on where you are. But no matter the title, they're all about boosting mental well-being.
- **Finding Your Fit:** When you're looking for help, think about what issues you're grappling with and the approach that feels right. A chat with your regular doc or research can point you toward the mental health pro that matches your needs.

So, whether it's a psychologist, therapist, or counselor, these pros are here to help you navigate the mind's complex waters and find your way to better mental health.

PICKING THE RIGHT PRO FOR YOUR NEEDS: A HOW-TO GUIDE

Choosing the right professional, be it a doc, lawyer, accountant, plumber, or another expert, is important. It's a decision that can make or break your project or service experience. So, how do you make sure you're picking the right person for the job? Here's a step-by-step guide:

Figure Out What You Need:

- Start by getting crystal clear about what you're looking for. What's your goal? Any specific skills or experiences you need? Nail down these details first.

Do Your Homework:

- Time to hit the books (or the web)! Research professionals in your area. Ask folks you trust for recommendations and check out online reviews to see what others are saying.

Qualifications and Experience Check:

- Make sure they've got the right credentials. Are they licensed? Accredited? Also, experience counts – someone who's tackled similar stuff before knows their way around.

Reputation Matters:

- You want someone with a solid rep. Look for rave reviews and happy clients. Steer clear of anyone with a laundry list of complaints or disciplinary woes.

Communication is Key:

- A pro who can't talk shop clearly won't do you much good. In your early chats, gauge how well they listen, explain things, and respond to your questions.

Money Talk:

- Budget's important, but don't let it be your only guide. Get quotes, compare, and see who offers the best bang for your buck.

Meet and Greet:

- Set up consultations or interviews. It's your chance to ask questions, discuss your needs, and see if they're the right fit.

Trust Your Instincts:

- Sometimes, you just gotta go with your gut. If something feels off, maybe check out other options.

References, Please:

- Ask for and actually call up their references. What was their work like? How's their professionalism? Did they leave the clients happy?

Reflect on Your Options:

- After doing all the legwork, step back. Think over your options carefully before choosing.

Remember, picking the right professional is all about doing your homework, checking their creds, weighing their rep, ensuring they're easy to talk to, considering costs, consulting with them, trusting your gut, checking references, and then sitting back and thinking it over. With these steps, you're all set to find the best person for your needs!

MAKING THE MOST OF PROFESSIONAL GUIDANCE: HOW TO BE AN ACTIVE PARTICIPANT

WHEN YOU'RE GETTING advice or coaching from a professional, like a career coach, mentor, or counselor, it's a big deal. To get the most out of it, you've got to be more than just a listener; you've got to dive in and be part of the process. Here's how you can do just that:

Set Your Goals Straight:

- Kick things off by knowing what you want to achieve. Want to climb the career ladder? Improve your skills? Tackle a challenge? Clear goals will steer the whole thing in the right direction.

Open Up:

- The more open and honest you are, the better. Your strengths, weaknesses, dreams, fears - spill it. This gives the pro a full picture and helps them tailor their advice right for you.

Really Listen:

- Pay close attention to what your guide says. Ask questions if you're puzzled by something. Active listening means you're tuned in and digesting the advice.

Own It:

- Remember, you're the captain of your ship. The pro can guide you, but you've got to do the sailing. Take charge of your actions and decisions.

Feedback is Your Friend:

- Ask for feedback and brace yourself for some honest-to-goodness advice. Constructive criticism? That's gold for your growth.

Be Proactive:

- Don't just sit back and wait for answers to come to you. Dig around, network, and stay on top of trends in your field. Show that you're serious about growing.

Keep the Lines Open:

- Regular catch-ups with your pro are key. Let them know how you're doing, talk about any roadblocks, and get their take when you need it.

Take Time to Reflect:

- Now and then, step back and see how far you've come. Are you hitting your goals? What's working and what's not? Reflecting helps you stay on track and make any tweaks needed.

Active participation in your professional development means you're not just going along for the ride; you're driving the car. Dive in, engage, and take ownership, and you'll squeeze every bit of goodness out of that professional guidance!

SECTION FOURTEEN WRAP-UP:

KEY POINTS:

RECOGNIZING the Need for Professional Help and Guidance

- **Mental Health Matters:** Seek a therapist for conditions like anxiety or depression.
- **Life's Big Hurdles:** Consider a career coach or grief counselor for major life changes.
- **Personal Growth Goals:** A life coach or career counselor can help achieve personal and professional ambitions.

Researching and Finding Reliable Professionals

- **Expert Insight:** Professionals offer specialized knowledge and experience.
- **Fresh Eyes:** External perspective for fair advice.
- **Skill and Speed:** Professionals provide efficient and effective solutions.
- **The Right Contacts:** Access to a network of resources and opportunities.

- **Playing It Safe:** Avoid pitfalls with expert guidance.
- **Level Up:** Enhance personal skills through professional advice.

Tackling the Stigma of Asking for Help

- **Understanding Mental Health:** Professionals provide clarity and strategies for mental wellness.
- **Safe Space to Talk:** Judgment-free environment for open communication.
- **Boosting Overall Well-being:** Addressing mental health issues improves life quality.
- **Effective Mental Health Tools:** Access to proven therapies and treatments.
- **Strength in Reaching Out:** Overcoming stigma by acknowledging the power of professional help.

Navigating the Mental Health Pro Scene

- **Psychologists:** Offer assessments and therapy with high qualifications.
- **Therapists:** Provide talking therapies for individuals, couples, or groups.
- **Counselors:** Focus on specific areas like mental health, addiction, or careers.
- **Choosing the Right Professional:** Match the expert to specific mental health needs.

Picking the Right Pro for Your Needs

- **Define Your Requirements:** Clearly identify what you need from a professional.
- **Do Research:** Look for qualified and experienced professionals with good reviews.
- **Check Qualifications and Experience:** Ensure they have the necessary credentials.

- **Assess Communication Skills:** Choose someone who communicates effectively.
- **Consider Budget and Get Quotes:** Align choice with financial considerations.
- **Meet and Discuss:** Conduct interviews or consultations to gauge compatibility.
- **Trust Instincts and Check References:** Validate your choice through references and intuition.

Making the Most of Professional Guidance

- **Set Clear Goals:** Establish goals for professional guidance.
- **Be Open and Honest:** Share comprehensive personal information for tailored advice.
- **Actively Listen and Engage:** Fully absorb and question the advice given.
- **Take Responsibility:** Own your decisions and actions based on guidance.
- **Seek and Use Feedback:** Embrace constructive criticism for personal growth.
- **Be Proactive and Network:** Show initiative in personal development.
- **Regular Communication:** Keep your professional advisor updated.
- **Reflect on Progress:** Regularly evaluate your growth and adjust goals as needed.

ACTION ITEMS:

Seeking Professional Help and Guidance

- **Consult a Therapist:** If experiencing mental health issues, schedule an appointment with a therapist.
- **Find a Career Coach:** For career challenges, seek guidance from a career coach.

- **Hire a Personal Growth Expert:** Engage with a life coach for personal development.

Researching and Finding Reliable Professionals

- **Research Online:** Look up professionals in your area and read reviews.
- **Verify Credentials:** Check the qualifications and experiences of potential professionals.
- **Seek Referrals:** Ask friends or colleagues for recommendations.

Tackling the Stigma of Asking for Help

- **Educate Yourself:** Understand the importance of mental health and how professional help can benefit.
- **Openly Discuss Mental Health:** Normalize conversations about seeking professional help.

Navigating the Mental Health Pro Scene

- **Identify Your Needs:** Decide whether a psychologist, therapist, or counselor suits your requirements.
- **Consult Your Doctor:** Get referrals from your primary care doctor.

Picking the Right Pro for Your Needs

- **List Potential Professionals:** Create a list of potential candidates based on research.
- **Conduct Interviews:** Arrange consultations with your shortlisted professionals.
- **Make a Decision:** Choose the professional that best aligns with your needs and comfort.

Making the Most of Professional Guidance

- **Prepare for Sessions:** Outline your goals and concerns before appointments.
- **Actively Participate:** Engage in sessions, ask questions, and apply advice.
- **Regularly Evaluate:** Assess your progress and adjust goals with your professional advisor.

By following these key points and action items, you can effectively leverage professional help and guidance for your personal and professional development.

In Our Next Section:

In our next section, we'll dive into the transformative power of reflection and continuous self-improvement. Life's journey is peppered with various challenges, but it's the art of looking back and drawing wisdom from our experiences that propels us forward. We'll explore how regular self-reflection not only enhances our understanding of personal triumphs and trials but also fine-tunes our future strategies. This process is important for anyone aiming to navigate life's complexities with grace and effectiveness. Reflection is the mirror that reveals our true resilience and potential, guiding us to become better versions of ourselves.

We'll tackle the ever-important idea of continuous self-improvement. In a world that's constantly evolving, staying static is not an option. We must embrace the pursuit of learning, growing, and adapting as integral parts of our personal and professional lives. This section will provide practical tips and strategies to foster a mindset of continuous improvement, making sure you're always ready to meet the demands of changing circumstances and new challenges. Get ready to start a journey of perpetual growth, where each step, no matter how small, is a leap toward your ultimate goals. Stay motivated, stay curious, and most important, stay on the path of self-improvement.

◞◟

SECTION FIFTEEN: CELEBRATING AND LEARNING FROM SUCCESSFULLY OVERCOMING CHALLENGES

INTRODUCTION TO EMBRACING AND LEARNING FROM CHALLENGES

HEY, let's talk about something we all face – challenges. They're part of life, right? But here's the cool part: overcoming them can be a real game-changer, both personally and professionally. It's all about not just getting past these hurdles but also celebrating our wins and soaking up all the lessons they offer. This approach helps us grow, become more resilient, and get the best out of tough times.

Facing the Challenges: Every bump in the road, big or small, shapes us. The key isn't just to get past these obstacles but to make them count. Each challenge we conquer is a victory worth celebrating.

Why Celebrate? Celebrating our successes is like giving ourselves a high-five. It's recognizing the hard work and determination we've poured in. This not only boosts our confidence but also pumps us up for the next round of challenges. It's a moment of "Hey, I did it!" that reminds us we can tackle anything that comes our way.

Learning from the Experience: Every challenge is a learning opportunity. It's a chance to look back and think, "What worked? What didn't? What can I do better next time?" Maybe we pick up a new skill, get better at solving problems, or learn something new about ourselves.

These insights are golden – they prepare us for future hurdles and help us avoid making the same oopsies again.

Inspiring Others: Our victories aren't just about us. They can light a spark for others too. When people see us overcoming obstacles, it's like saying, "You got this too!" We can share our stories, the strategies that helped us, and become a cheerleader for others facing their own challenges.

Wrap-Up: So, celebrating and learning from our successes in overcoming challenges? It's powerful stuff. It's about growing, bouncing back stronger, and keeping a positive vibe. It's about appreciating our progress, learning from the journey, and helping others along the way. Embracing challenges as chances for growth turns tough times into stepping stones toward success and a more rewarding life. Let's take on those challenges and make the most of them!

PERSONAL ANECDOTES AND STORIES OF INDIVIDUALS WHO HAVE FACED AND CONQUERED SIGNIFICANT CHALLENGES

NOTE: These case studies are fictional and are provided for illustrative purposes only.

Introduction:

In life, we often come across individuals who have battled through daunting obstacles and emerged stronger, wiser, and triumphant. These stories of resilience serve as a testament to the human spirit, reminding us that even the most significant challenges can be conquered with determination, courage, and unwavering belief. Here, we share personal anecdotes of remarkable individuals who defied the odds and turned adversity into opportunities for growth and transformation.

OVERCOMING THE ODDS: STORIES OF TRIUMPH AND RESILIENCE

Part 1: Redemption Against Addiction

Case Study One: Jennifer's Journey: From the Depths of Addiction to a Life of Sobriety

Background: Jennifer, a young woman in her early thirties, had been battling addiction since her late teens. Growing up in a high-pressure environment, she first turned to substances to cope with stress and anxiety. Over the years, her occasional use turned into dependency, affecting her health, relationships, and career.

Challenge: Jennifer's life was overshadowed by the relentless grip of addiction. She lost her job, faced financial hardships, and her relationships with family and friends deteriorated. The turning point came when she faced legal troubles due to her substance abuse.

Response: Realizing the gravity of her situation, Jennifer decided to seek help. She enrolled in a rehabilitation program, which was the first step toward her journey to sobriety. The road to recovery was fraught with challenges, including withdrawal symptoms, the battle against cravings, and rebuilding her broken life.

Strategy:

1. Rehabilitation Program: Jennifer underwent a comprehensive rehabilitation program, which included detoxification, therapy, and counseling. This helped her understand the root causes of her addiction and develop coping mechanisms.

2. Support Systems: She actively sought support from support groups, such as Alcoholics Anonymous (AA). Engaging with individuals who faced similar struggles gave her a sense of community and understanding.

3. Personal Development: Jennifer took up activities that promoted mental and physical well-being, such as yoga and meditation. These practices helped her manage stress and anxiety, which were triggers for her substance use.

4. Rebuilding Relationships: She worked on mending relationships with her family and friends, which was important for her emotional support system. Open communication and therapy sessions helped rebuild trust and understanding with her loved ones.

5. Career Rehabilitation: Jennifer also focused on her professional life. She started volunteering and eventually found a part-time job. This gradual approach helped her rebuild her confidence and sense of purpose.

Results: After two years of continuous effort and dedication, Jennifer achieved sobriety. She transformed her life from the depths of addiction to one of balance and health. Her relationships were restored, and she found steady employment in a field she was passionate about.

Conclusion: Jennifer's journey is a powerful testament to the human spirit's resilience. It highlights the importance of seeking help, having a strong support system, and the willingness to change. Her story serves as an inspiration to others facing similar challenges, proving that it's possible to turn adversity into an opportunity for growth and transformation. Her life, now filled with purpose and sobriety, stands as a beacon of hope and a reminder that even the most daunting obstacles can be overcome.

Case Study Two: Michael's Battle: Overcoming Substance Abuse and Building a Joyful Future

Background: Michael, a 40-year-old man, faced a tumultuous journey battling substance abuse. His struggle began in his mid-twenties, initially as a way to escape personal and professional pressures. However, what started as casual use, spiraled into a debilitating addiction that consumed a significant part of his life.

Challenge: Michael's addiction led to severe consequences. He lost his job as a marketing executive, his relationships with family and friends became strained, and his physical and mental health deteriorated rapidly. His life reached a critical point when he was hospitalized due to an overdose, which served as a stark wake-up call.

Response: Determined to reclaim his life, Michael took the courageous step to enroll in a rehabilitation program. He committed wholeheartedly to the program, embracing every part of the recovery process.

Strategy:

1.   **Comprehensive Rehabilitation:** Michael's recovery journey began with a medically supervised detox, followed by intensive therapy. He participated in individual and group therapy sessions, which helped him confront and understand the underlying issues fueling his addiction.

2.   **Building a Support Network:** Recognizing the importance of support, Michael joined various support groups where he connected with others sharing similar experiences. These groups provided a platform for encouragement and accountability, which were critical in his recovery.

3.   **Lifestyle Changes:** To replace the void left by substance abuse, Michael adopted healthier lifestyle habits. He engaged in regular exercise, joined a local sports club, and took up hobbies he had previously abandoned, such as painting and hiking.

4.   **Restoring Relationships:** Michael worked earnestly to rebuild the relationships that were damaged due to his addiction. He sought forgiveness and understanding from his loved ones and actively worked on regaining their trust.

5.   **Career Rehabilitation:** Michael gradually re-entered the professional world. At first, he took on freelance projects to rebuild his portfolio and eventually secured a full-time position in a smaller firm, where he could manage his stress levels more effectively.

Results: After a year of persistent effort, Michael achieved sobriety. His life underwent a complete transformation – he mended his relationships, regained his health, and established a stable career. He also became an active speaker in substance abuse awareness programs, sharing his story to inspire and help others.

Conclusion: Michael's journey is a powerful illustration of overcoming adversity through resilience and determination. His story underscores the importance of seeking help, the strength found in community, and the power of self-belief in changing one's life. Michael's life, once overshadowed by addiction, is now filled with purpose, health, and joy. His experience serves as a beacon of hope for many, proving that with the right support and mindset, it's possible to turn even the darkest moments into opportunities for growth and a brighter future.

PART 2: NAVIGATING THROUGH PHYSICAL LIMITATIONS

Case Study Three: Sarah's Triumph: From Paralyzed to Paralympics

Background: Sarah, a vibrant 30-year-old athlete, experienced a life-altering accident at the age of 22, which left her paralyzed from the waist down. A promising track star, her dreams seemed shattered in an instant. However, her story didn't end there; it was merely the beginning of a new chapter.

Challenge: Post-accident, Sarah grappled with the harsh reality of her physical limitations. The world she knew - full of races, training, and physical prowess - seemed like a distant memory. She faced not only the physical challenge of navigating life in a wheelchair but also the mental and emotional battle of redefining her identity and purpose.

Response: Sarah's journey to recovery and transformation was fueled by her indomitable spirit. Refusing to be defined by her disability, she sought to find new ways to embrace her passion for athletics.

Strategy:

1. **Physical Rehabilitation:** Intensive physical therapy was the first step. Sarah dedicated countless hours to strengthening her upper body and learning to navigate her new physical reality with grace and strength.

2. **Mental Health Support:** Recognizing the importance of mental well-being, Sarah sought counseling to help her process her trauma

and rebuild her self-confidence. She learned to reframe her situation, focusing on possibilities rather than limitations.

3. **Discovering Para-Sports:** Sarah discovered the world of para-sports, which opened a new realm of opportunities. She was drawn to wheelchair racing and para-rowing, sports that resonated with her love for speed and competition.

4. **Training and Dedication:** With renewed purpose, Sarah started rigorous training, adapting her athletic skills to her new discipline. She found coaches who specialized in training para-athletes, which was instrumental in her development.

5. **Community and Support:** Joining a community of para-athletes, Sarah found camaraderie and support. She formed bonds with individuals who shared similar experiences, which provided motivation and strength.

6. **Setting New Goals:** Sarah set her sights on competing in the Paralympics, channeling her energy and focusing on achieving this new dream.

Results: After years of dedication and hard work, Sarah qualified for the Paralympics. Her participation was not just a personal victory but also a symbol of resilience and hope. She won medals, but more important, she won the hearts of many, inspiring others to rise above their circumstances.

Conclusion: Sarah's journey from being paralyzed to becoming a Paralympian is a remarkable testament to the human spirit's resilience. Her story exemplifies how daunting challenges can transform into opportunities for growth and triumph. Sarah's life, once overshadowed by a tragic accident, is now a beacon of inspiration, showing that physical limitations do not define one's capabilities or dampen the spirit of competition and the will to succeed. Her triumph at the Paralympics stands as a powerful reminder of what can be achieved with courage, determination, and unwavering belief in oneself.

Case Study Four: Alex's Unwavering Spirit: Living Life to the Fullest with a Disability

Background: Alex, a young and energetic individual, faced a life-changing event at the age of 15, which caused the loss of his lower limbs. An accident that could have ended any teenager's dreams became the start of Alex's extraordinary journey of resilience and determination.

Challenge: The accident left Alex navigating a world that was not only physically challenging but also filled with societal barriers and stereotypes about disability. He faced the daunting task of relearning basic movements and activities, while also coping with the emotional and psychological impact of his sudden disability.

Response: Refusing to let his disability define his life, Alex chose to see his situation as a unique opportunity to inspire and effect change. His response to his disability was characterized by an unwavering spirit and a positive outlook on life.

Strategy:

1. **Physical Adaptation and Rehabilitation:** Alex began with intensive physical therapy, focusing on mastering the use of prosthetics and a wheelchair. He worked tirelessly to regain his independence in mobility.

2. **Embracing Adaptive Sports:** Alex discovered adaptive sports, which reignited his passion for physical activity. He dug into sports like wheelchair basketball and para-swimming, finding joy and a sense of accomplishment in these new challenges.

3. **Advocacy and Raising Awareness:** Alex became an advocate for people with disabilities. He used his experience to educate others, raise awareness about accessibility issues, and promote inclusivity in sports and other areas of society.

4. **Pursuing Education and Career Goals:** Determined to not let his disability hinder his education and career aspirations, Alex continued his studies, focusing on subjects he was passionate about. He also

explored different career paths where he could use his experience to make a difference.

5.   **Building a Support Network:** Recognizing the importance of community support, Alex connected with others with similar experiences. He joined support groups and actively participated in community events related to disability and advocacy.

6.   **Setting New Life Goals:** Alex set ambitious goals for himself, both in his personal life and in his advocacy work. He aimed to participate in adaptive sports at a competitive level and dreamed of creating more accessible environments for people with disabilities.

Results: Alex's journey led him to many achievements in both his personal and advocacy efforts. In sports, he won several medals in national competitions, inspiring others with his athleticism and spirit. His advocacy work contributed to significant improvements in local accessibility policies and raised considerable awareness about the challenges faced by people with disabilities.

Conclusion: Alex's story is a powerful example of how physical limitations do not restrict one's ability to live a fulfilling and impactful life. His unwavering spirit in the face of adversity has not only let him achieve personal goals but has also made him a beacon of inspiration for others. Alex's journey shows that with determination, courage, and a positive mindset, any challenge can be transformed into an opportunity for growth, making a lasting impact on both the individual and the community.

PART 3: TRANSFORMING PAIN INTO PURPOSE

Case Study Five: From Trauma to Transformation: Emma's Journey of Healing and Advocacy

Background: Emma, a vibrant young woman in her twenties, faced a life-altering experience that would challenge her physically, emotionally, and mentally. A victim of a violent assault, Emma grappled with trauma that threatened to derail her life's trajectory.

Challenge: The assault left Emma struggling with deep-seated trauma, affecting her mental health and daily functioning. She battled feelings of fear, anger, and helplessness, while also dealing with the physical aftermath of the attack. The incident posed a significant challenge to her sense of safety, trust in others, and her life plans.

Response: Instead of succumbing to her circumstances, Emma chose to channel her pain into purpose. She started a journey of healing and transformation, turning her personal tragedy into a crusade for change and advocacy.

Strategy:

1.   **Seeking Professional Help:** Recognizing the need for support, Emma sought therapy to address her trauma. She worked with a counselor specializing in trauma recovery, helping her process her emotions and develop coping strategies.

2.   **Engaging in Self-Care:** Emma understood the importance of self-care in her recovery process. She engaged in activities that nurtured her physical and mental well-being, such as yoga, meditation, and art therapy. These activities gave her a sense of peace and an outlet for expression.

3.   **Finding Community Support:** Emma reached out to support groups for survivors of violence. These groups provided a safe space for sharing experiences and offered mutual support, helping Emma realize she was not alone in her journey.

4.   **Advocacy and Awareness Raising:** Motivated by her experiences, Emma became an advocate for survivors of violence. She started participating in awareness campaigns, sharing her story to educate others about the impact of trauma and the importance of support for survivors.

5.   **Pursuing Education and Advocacy Work:** Emma decided to further her education in psychology, aiming to specialize in trauma

counseling. Her goal was to help others in healing from similar experiences.

6. **Creating a Platform for Change:** Emma leveraged social media to create a platform where she could reach a wider audience. She shared resources, personal insights, and advocated for policy changes related to violence against women.

Results: Emma's journey of healing and transformation had a profound impact. Not only did she make significant strides in her own recovery, but she also became a beacon of hope for other survivors. Her advocacy work led to collaborations with local organizations, contributing to the development of better support systems for survivors of violence. Emma's educational pursuit in psychology positioned her to become a skilled counselor, dedicated to helping others navigate their paths to healing.

Conclusion: Emma's story illustrates the incredible power of transforming personal pain into purpose. Her resilience in the face of trauma, combined with her dedication to advocacy and helping others, transformed a personal tragedy into a journey of healing, growth, and meaningful impact. Emma's experience serves as a testament to the strength of the human spirit and the potential to create positive change out of life's most challenging moments.

Case Study Six: David's Mission: Rebuilding Lives After Natural Disasters

Background: David, a civil engineer in his mid-thirties, experienced a profound turning point in his life following a devastating hurricane that struck his hometown. The disaster caused significant destruction, leaving many residents homeless and in despair.

Challenge: The hurricane's aftermath was a scene of chaos and heartbreak. David saw the loss and suffering of his community, including close friends and family. The scale of destruction overwhelmed the local resources, creating a dire need for reconstruction and support.

Response: Moved by the plight of his community, David used his skills and knowledge to make a real difference. He started a mission to help rebuild his town, focusing not only on the physical reconstruction of structures but also on supporting the emotional recovery of the residents.

Strategy:

1. **Community Mobilization:** David began by organizing a team of local volunteers, rallying the community to participate in the rebuilding efforts. He believed that involving residents in the process would foster a sense of empowerment and collective healing.

2. **Collaboration with Experts:** Recognizing the need for specialized skills, David contacted fellow engineers, architects, and urban planners to volunteer their services. He helped with workshops and planning sessions to design resilient and sustainable rebuilding strategies.

3. **Securing Funding and Resources:** David started fundraising campaigns and collaborated with NGOs and governmental agencies to secure the necessary funding and resources. He advocated for the community, making sure the rebuilding efforts were adequately supported.

4. **Innovative Building Solutions:** Utilizing his engineering background, David introduced innovative and cost-effective building solutions. He focused on constructing resilient structures that could withstand future natural disasters, thus reducing long-term risks.

5. **Psychological Support Programs:** Understanding the emotional impact of the disaster, David partnered with mental health professionals to provide counseling and support programs for the affected residents. He emphasized the importance of addressing the psychological well-being of the community alongside the physical rebuilding.

6. **Education and Preparedness Training:** To prepare for future disasters, David organized educational programs and emergency preparedness training for the community. He aimed to build a culture of resilience and awareness, empowering residents with the knowledge and skills to respond effectively in emergencies.

Results: David's mission transformed the face of his community. The rebuilding efforts not only restored homes and infrastructure but also rejuvenated the spirit of the town. His innovative approaches to construction led to safer, more resilient buildings. The community became more united and prepared, with residents participating in disaster preparedness programs. David's work drew attention from national organizations, leading to further collaborations and support for disaster resilience initiatives.

Conclusion: David's story is a remarkable example of how individual initiative, coupled with community collaboration, can turn the tide in the wake of adversity. His ability to transform pain into purpose not only rebuilt his town physically but also healed and strengthened the community's spirit. David's mission highlights the incredible impact of resilience, determination, and the power of collective action in overcoming even the most daunting challenges.

PART 4: RISING ABOVE MENTAL HEALTH STRUGGLES

Case Study Seven: Amy's Resilience: From Darkness to Mental Health Awareness

Background: Amy, a young professional in her late twenties, faced a formidable challenge when she was diagnosed with severe depression and anxiety. Her journey began during a stressful period at work, compounded by personal struggles that seemed insurmountable.

Challenge: Amy's mental health struggles significantly affected her daily life. She grappled with persistent feelings of hopelessness and anxiety, leading to social withdrawal and a decline in work performance. The stigma surrounding mental health in her community and workplace made it difficult for her to seek help or find understanding.

Response: Recognizing the severity of her condition, Amy took control of her life. She started a journey of healing and self-discovery, determined to overcome her struggles and help others facing similar challenges.

Strategy:

1. **Seeking Professional Help:** Amy's first step was to seek professional help. She began therapy and was prescribed medication to manage her symptoms. Regular counseling sessions gave her the tools to understand and cope with her mental health issues.

2. **Lifestyle Changes:** Amy realized the importance of a holistic approach to her recovery. She adopted a healthier lifestyle, including regular exercise, a balanced diet, and adequate sleep. She also practiced mindfulness and meditation to help manage her anxiety.

3. **Building a Support System:** Understanding the power of community, Amy contacted friends and family, educating them about her struggles. She also joined support groups where she found comfort and understanding among peers with similar experiences.

4. **Advocacy and Awareness:** As she navigated through her recovery, Amy became passionate about mental health advocacy. She started a blog to share her journey and spread awareness about mental health issues, aiming to break the stigma and encourage others to seek help.

5. **Volunteering and Community Involvement:** Amy began volunteering with mental health organizations. She participated in workshops, spoke at events, and collaborated with mental health professionals to provide resources and support to those struggling.

6. **Educational Pursuits:** Inspired by her own experience, Amy decided to further her education in psychology. She aimed to deepen her understanding of mental health and contribute more effectively to the field.

Results: Amy's journey from darkness to mental health awareness marked a significant transformation. Her advocacy and outreach efforts helped many individuals feel less alone in their struggles. Her blog became a beacon of hope and a resourceful guide for those dealing with similar issues. Amy's involvement in community projects and educational pursuits positioned her as a respected voice in mental health advocacy.

Conclusion: Amy's story is a powerful testament to the human spirit's resilience. By turning her personal struggle into an opportunity for growth and transformation, she not only bettered her own life but also positively affected the lives of many others. Her journey underscores the importance of seeking help, building a supportive community, and raising awareness about mental health. Amy's resilience reminds us that even in the face of great adversity, it is possible to emerge stronger, wiser, and with a renewed purpose.

Case Study Eight: Mark's Journey - Battling Depression and Finding Inner Peace

Background: Mark, a middle-aged engineer, faced a profound challenge when he was diagnosed with clinical depression. His struggle began silently, overshadowed by a demanding career and societal expectations to always seem strong and composed.

Challenge: Mark's depression manifested in intense feelings of sadness, loss of interest in activities he once enjoyed, and a pervasive sense of hopelessness. These symptoms not only affected his personal life but also his performance at work. The stigma associated with mental health, particularly for men in his community, made it difficult for him to acknowledge his struggle and seek help.

Response: Realizing that his condition was affecting every part of his life, Mark decided to confront his depression head-on. He committed to a journey of healing, self-discovery, and advocacy, determined to reclaim his life and help others facing similar battles.

Strategy:

1. **Professional Help:** Mark's first critical step was to acknowledge his need for professional help. He began therapy and worked with a psychiatrist to find the right medication to manage his symptoms, a process that required patience and persistence.

2.   **Building a Supportive Network:** He opened up to his family and close friends, slowly dismantling the walls he had built around his struggles. Their support gave him a safety net and a sounding board for his experiences.

3.   **Lifestyle Adjustments:** Mark incorporated exercise into his daily routine, embraced a healthier diet, and established a consistent sleep schedule. He discovered these changes, while small, significantly affected his mood and energy levels.

4.   **Mindfulness and Meditation:** To find inner peace, Mark turned to mindfulness and meditation. These practices helped him develop greater awareness of his thoughts and emotions, letting him manage his depressive symptoms more effectively.

5.   **Community Engagement:** Mark joined support groups for individuals dealing with depression. Sharing his experiences and hearing others' stories helped him feel less isolated in his journey and provided a sense of community.

6.   **Advocacy:** As he became more comfortable with his story, Mark began to advocate for mental health awareness in his workplace. He organized workshops and shared his journey, contributing to a more open and supportive work environment.

7.   **Creative Outlets:** Mark rediscovered his passion for photography, a hobby he had neglected. This creative outlet gave him a sense of accomplishment and joy, important elements in his healing process.

Results: Mark's journey was transformative. Not only did he find inner peace and regain control over his life, but he also inspired others to acknowledge and confront their mental health struggles. His advocacy at work led to the implementation of mental health resources and support systems for employees.

Conclusion: Mark's story is a powerful example of how confronting and managing mental health struggles can lead to personal growth and societal impact. His journey underscores the importance of seeking professional help, building a supportive network, embracing self-care practices, and advocating for mental health awareness. By turning his battle with depression into an opportunity for transformation and advocacy, Mark not only improved his own life but also became a beacon of hope and resilience for others.

PART 5: CONQUERING PROFESSIONAL CHALLENGES

Case Study Nine: Alice's Dream - Overcoming Gender Bias in the Tech Industry

Background: Alice, a talented software developer, had always aspired to make her mark in the technology industry. Despite her passion and knowledge, she found herself confronted with significant gender bias, a challenge pervasive in her field.

Challenge: Alice encountered skepticism about her technical abilities purely based on her gender. She often found herself overlooked for key projects and promotions, despite her clear skills and contributions. The underrepresentation of women in tech further exacerbated the issue, leaving her with few role models or mentors.

Response: Determined to overcome these barriers, Alice started a journey to establish her place in the tech world and advocate for gender equality within the industry.

Strategy:

1. **Skill Enhancement:** Alice committed to continuous learning to hone her skills. She went to workshops, pursued certifications, and stayed abreast of the latest technological advancements, ensuring her knowledge was undeniable.

2. **Networking:** Understanding the power of connections, Alice actively networked within the industry. She went to tech meetups, joined professional groups, and participated in tech forums, building a supportive network of peers and allies.

3.   **Mentorship:** Alice sought mentors who provided guidance and support. She also became a mentor to younger women entering the field, sharing her experiences and advice.

4.   **Raising Awareness:** Alice started a blog discussing her experiences as a woman in tech. Her insightful posts about gender bias in the workplace gained attention, sparking meaningful conversations in the industry.

5.   **Public Speaking:** She leveraged opportunities to speak at industry conferences and panels, positioning herself as a knowledgeable and influential figure in the tech community.

6.   **Advocacy:** Alice collaborated with organizations promoting diversity in tech. She participated in initiatives aimed at encouraging more women to pursue careers in technology and advocating for equitable practices in workplaces.

Results: Alice's efforts paid off. Her enhanced skills and industry presence led to recognition within her company. She was eventually promoted to a leadership role, where she put policies into practice to ensure a more inclusive and diverse workplace. Her advocacy work contributed to broader industry conversations about gender bias in tech, inspiring many companies to reassess their diversity and inclusion strategies.

Conclusion: Alice's journey is a testament to her resilience and determination in the face of gender bias in the tech industry. Her story highlights the importance of skill development, networking, mentorship, and advocacy in overcoming professional challenges. Through her efforts, Alice not only achieved her own career goals but also paved the way for future generations of women in technology. Her story serves as an inspiration, showing that with courage and perseverance, it's possible to challenge the status quo and drive meaningful change in even the most challenging environments.

Case Study Ten: Andrew's Persistence - From Laid-off to Successful Entrepreneur

Background: Andrew, a dedicated marketing professional, faced an unexpected career setback when he was laid off from his long-term job due to company restructuring. This event marked a critical turning point in his life.

Challenge: Finding himself suddenly unemployed, Andrew grappled with feelings of uncertainty and self-doubt. The job market was competitive, and his attempts at finding similar employment were met with repeated rejections.

Response: Instead of succumbing to despair, Andrew saw this as an opportunity to reshape his professional journey. He decided to pursue his long-held dream of starting his own business.

Strategy:

1. **Self-Assessment:** Andrew took time to reflect on his skills, passions, and experiences. He identified digital marketing as a niche where he could leverage his knowledge.

2. **Market Research:** He conducted thorough research to understand market needs and identify potential opportunities. This helped him carve out a unique proposition for his business.

3. **Learning and Development:** Andrew updated his skills through online courses and certifications, particularly focusing on digital marketing trends and entrepreneurship.

4. **Building a Network:** He used his existing professional network and actively went to industry events to build new connections, seek advice, and gain mentors.

5. **Business Plan Development:** Andrew crafted a detailed business plan, outlining his business model, target market, and growth strategies. This plan served as a roadmap for his entrepreneurial journey.

6. **Starting Small:** He launched his business from his home office, keeping overheads low while focusing on building a client base.

7. **Marketing and Brand Building:** Leveraging his marketing knowledge, Andrew developed a strong online presence for his business, using social media and content marketing to attract clients.

8. **Adapting and Innovating:** Andrew remained adaptable, continually evolving his strategies in response to market feedback and industry trends.

Results: Andrew's persistence and strategic approach bore fruit. His business gradually gained traction, attracting a diverse range of clients. As his reputation grew, so did his business, letting him hire a team and expand his services. His entrepreneurial success also led him to become a sought-after speaker and mentor for aspiring entrepreneurs.

Conclusion: Andrew's journey from being laid off to becoming a successful entrepreneur is a powerful illustration of resilience in the face of professional challenges. It underscores the importance of self-reflection, continuous learning, strategic planning, and network building in overcoming adversity. Andrew's story is a beacon of inspiration, showing that with determination and a proactive approach, it's possible to transform obstacles into stepping stones for success and personal fulfillment.

PART 6: DEFYING CULTURAL BARRIERS

Case Study Eleven: Mona's Courage - Breaking Free from the Shackles of Oppression

Background: Mona grew up in a culturally conservative community where women's roles were traditionally defined, and their opportunities for education and career advancement were severely limited. From a young age, she aspired to break free from these constraints and pave her own path.

Challenge: Mona faced significant resistance from her community and even her family. Her aspirations for higher education and a professional career were met with skepticism and disapproval. She was constantly reminded of the cultural expectations and limitations placed on women in her society.

Response: Undeterred by these challenges, Mona was determined to pursue her dreams. She believed that education was her gateway to freedom and empowerment.

Strategy:

1. **Pursuing Education:** Despite the odds, Mona worked hard to excel academically. She earned a scholarship to go to a university, a rare achievement for women in her community.

2. **Building Support Networks:** Mona sought allies and mentors who supported her ambitions. She connected with organizations that advocate for women's rights and education.

3. **Cultural Negotiation:** She engaged in dialogues with her family and community leaders, highlighting the importance of women's education and empowerment. Mona respectfully challenged traditional norms while showing sensitivity to her cultural background.

4. **Empowering Others:** As she pursued her education, Mona also began to mentor young girls in her community, encouraging them to aspire for more and helping them navigate similar challenges.

5. **Professional Success:** Armed with education and determination, Mona started a successful career. She used her platform to advocate for women's rights and education, becoming a role model for many.

6. **Community Engagement:** Despite her professional success, Mona remained actively involved in her community, using her influence to slowly bring about cultural change and greater acceptance of women's roles in society.

Results: Mona's journey was transformative not only for her but also for her community. Her achievements challenged long-held beliefs and opened doors for other women to follow. Her advocacy work led to greater awareness and gradual cultural shifts in her community's perception of women's roles.

Conclusion: Mona's story is a testament to the power of resilience, courage, and pursuing education in the face of cultural barriers. Her journey from a young girl in a conservative community to a successful professional and advocate for women's rights illustrates that breaking free from the shackles of oppression is possible. Mona's courage and determination have not only reshaped her life but have also paved the way for future generations of women in her community. Her story is an inspiration, showing that defying cultural barriers, while challenging, can lead to significant transformation and empowerment.

Case Study Twelve: Raj's Rebellion - Challenging Stereotypes for LGBTQ+ Acceptance

Background: Raj grew up in a traditional, conservative community where the LGBTQ+ community was not openly accepted or understood. From a young age, Raj struggled with his identity, knowing that his truth conflicted with the expectations and norms of his surroundings.

Challenge: Raj grappled with the internal conflict of being true to himself while fearing rejection from his family, friends, and community. He faced the daunting challenge of living in an environment where being LGBTQ+ was stigmatized and often met with hostility.

Response: Determined to embrace his identity and foster understanding and acceptance, Raj took a stand against the stereotypes and prejudices within his community.

Strategy:

1. **Self-Acceptance:** Raj's first step was to accept himself. He sought support from online communities and local LGBTQ+ groups, which helped him build confidence and resilience.

2. **Educating Others:** Understanding that ignorance was at the root of much prejudice, Raj began to educate those around him. He shared information, resources, and personal stories to demystify LGBTQ+ issues.

3. **Engaging in Dialogue:** Raj started open and respectful conversations with family and friends. He spoke about the importance of diversity, acceptance, and empathy, challenging deep-seated beliefs and encouraging a reevaluation of prejudices.

4. **Community Involvement:** Raj became actively involved in local LGBTQ+ advocacy groups. He organized events, workshops, and talks to increase visibility and promote understanding within the broader community.

5. **Role Model:** By living openly and authentically, Raj became a role model to others in similar situations. His courage and openness helped others in his community feel less isolated and more empowered to embrace their identities.

6. **Collaboration with Allies:** Raj collaborated with allies and supporters within and outside the LGBTQ+ community to strengthen his efforts. These partnerships helped amplify his message and reach a broader audience.

Results: Raj's efforts led to real changes in attitudes within his community. His family, initially hesitant, began to show support and understanding. His actions inspired others to challenge their preconceptions and fostered a more inclusive and accepting environment.

Conclusion: Raj's journey is a powerful example of how one individual can challenge cultural barriers and stereotypes to create change. His story highlights the importance of self-acceptance, education, open dialogue, and community involvement in the fight for LGBTQ+ acceptance. Through his resilience and determination, Raj not only transformed his own life but also paved the way for greater acceptance and inclusion in his community. His rebellion against cultural stereotypes stands as a beacon of hope and a call to action for those striving to overcome similar obstacles.

Chapter Conclusion:

These stories illustrate the indomitable spirit of individuals who have faced and conquered significant challenges. Through their strength, perseverance, and unwavering determination, they remind us that no matter how daunting our trials may seem, it is possible to rise above them. Their triumphs serve as beacons of hope and inspiration for all of us, encouraging us never to give up and to strive for greatness, even in the face of adversity.

~

CELEBRATING OUR WINS

LET's dive into why it's important to celebrate and recognize our own achievements. It's more than just throwing a party or patting ourselves on the back. It's about boosting our self-confidence and stoking that fire of motivation within us. Each time we cross a finish line, big or small, it's a chance to appreciate the journey and the hard work that got us there.

Why Celebrate, Anyway?

- **Boosts Confidence:** Every time we achieve something, it's like a high-five to our abilities and efforts. Celebrating these moments shines a light on our skills and strengths, making us feel more confident and ready to tackle what's next.
- **Brings Satisfaction:** There's a special joy in reaching a goal, right? Taking the time to celebrate lets us soak in that happiness and satisfaction. It's like savoring the flavor of success, which can be a huge mood booster and give us a positive outlook on things.
- **Inspires Others:** Our wins can be a beacon for others. Sharing our achievements can spark inspiration and hope in those

around us. It's a way of showing that, hey, with some grit and grind, they can reach their goals too.

- **Fuels Personal Growth:** Reflecting on our achievements isn't just about basking in glory. It's also a chance to look at what we learned, how we grew, and what we can do even better next time. It's about evolving and aiming higher with each win.

Wrapping Up: So, why make a big deal out of our achievements? Because it's more than just celebrating - it's about building up our confidence, enjoying our hard work's payoff, lighting the way for others, and setting the stage for even more growth. Every achievement, no matter the size, is a step forward in our journey. Let's give ourselves a round of applause and keep pushing for those wins!

EXPLORATION OF THE LESSONS AND INSIGHTS GAINED THROUGH OVERCOMING CHALLENGES

HEY, let's talk about how tackling challenges is like going to the gym for our character and mind. It's tough, sure, but the stuff we learn from these experiences? Priceless. Let's break down some of the big lessons we get from facing and overcoming hurdles in life.

Building Resilience:

- **Discovering Our Strength:** Every time we push through a tough spot, it's like we're showing ourselves just how resilient and strong we are. It's a reminder that even when the going gets tough, we have what it takes to keep moving forward.

Fueling Personal Growth:

- **Learning and Evolving:** Challenges force us out of our comfort zones. And guess what? That's exactly where we start learning new things and growing. Each challenge is a chance to pick up new skills and wisdom to carry forward.

Gaining Clarity on What Matters:

- **Priorities and Passions:** When we're in the thick of it, we often have to stop and think about what's important to us. It's like these challenges shine a spotlight on our true values and what we're passionate about.

Shifting Perspectives:

- **A New Way to Look at Things:** Overcoming challenges can change how we see life. We learn to view setbacks not just as roadblocks but as steps to something bigger and better. It's all about flipping the script and finding the growth in the grind.

The Power of Support:

- **Leaning on Others:** Tough times often remind us that we're not alone. We turn to friends, family, or mentors for a boost, and that's when we realize just how important it is to have a strong support network.

Finding Gratitude:

- **Appreciating the Good Stuff:** After we've weathered a storm, we often come out feeling more grateful for the good things in life. It's like overcoming challenges helps us appreciate the sunny days even more.

Briefly, every challenge we face and conquer is like a lesson in life's big classroom. We learn about our strengths, our values, and the importance of having good people in our corner. So, let's try to see these hurdles as chances to grow, learn, and become even better versions of ourselves. Bring it on, challenges! We're ready to learn and grow.

TECHNIQUES AND STRATEGIES FOR EFFECTIVELY NAVIGATING OBSTACLES AND LEARNING FROM THEM

Navigating **Life's Obstacles**

Hey there! Let's discuss handling life's hurdles, shall we? Whether it's stuff at work, in our personal lives, or those tough academic challenges, facing these head-on can actually be a chance to grow and learn. Here are cool ways to tackle these challenges and come out wiser on the other side.

Rocking a Growth Mindset:

- **View Challenges as Chances:** Start seeing these roadblocks as opportunities to level up. They're not just problems; they're your chance to grow and improve.

Stay Upbeat and Tough:

- **Keep Your Chin Up:** Keep that positive vibe rolling. Remember times you've aced it before, lean on your strengths, and don't forget your support crew. Resilience is key – every setback is a setup for a comeback.

Chop It Down to Size:

- **Tackle Bit by Bit:** Faced with a huge challenge? Break it down into smaller, easier chunks. This way, it's less overwhelming and you get to cheer for each little victory along the way.

Get a Fresh Take:

- **New Eyes, New Ideas:** Sometimes, seeing things from a different angle can help. Chat with mentors, friends, or colleagues for their thoughts – they might have the brainstorm you need.

Look Back to Leap Forward:

- **Past Wins as Guides:** Think back to how you've conquered challenges before. What worked? What didn't? Use those experiences as your secret weapon for what you're facing now.

Learn from the Oops Moments:

- **Failures as Lessons:** Okay, so sometimes things don't go as planned. Instead of getting stuck on the stumbles, think about what they can teach you. Adjust your game plan and you're good to go.

Self-Care is Key:

- **Take Care of You:** Navigating challenges can be draining. Make sure you're taking time for yourself – rest up, do what makes you happy, and keep stress at bay. A happy you is a more resilient you.

Helping Hands:

- **Ask Away:** There's no shame in reaching out when you need a hand. A mentor, coach, or your personal cheer squad can offer great advice and a much-needed morale boost.

Stay Curious and Flexible:

- **Keep Learning:** Every challenge is a chance to pick up something new. Keep an open mind, be ready to adapt, and keep adding to your skill set.

Party for Every Step:

- **Celebrate the Small Stuff:** Every little bit of progress is worth a mini-party. These celebrations boost your confidence and keep you pumped to take on the next part of the challenge.

So, let's remember – every obstacle is really a chance to learn, grow, and show just what we're made of. Bring 'em on!

HIGHLIGHTING THE ROLE OF RESILIENCE, PERSEVERANCE, AND GROWTH MINDSET IN OVERCOMING CHALLENGES

ALL RIGHT, let's talk about handling life's tough bits. You know, the personal hurdles, professional stumbles, or those out-of-the-blue snags. It's really how we deal with these tough times that shapes who we are. Now, there are three superheroes in this story: resilience, perseverance, and a growth mindset. Let me break it down for you.

Resilience - Your Bounce-Back Power:

- **Tough Times' Best Friend:** Think of resilience as your ability to get back up after life knocks you down. It's about facing those rough patches without losing your cool. Resilient folks see setbacks not as dead-ends, but as ramps to something better. They get that failure isn't the finale; it's just part of the journey to success. Building this resilience muscle means you can face life's curveballs and still keep your eye on the prize.

Perseverance - The Long-Haul Buddy:

- **Sticking It Out:** Perseverance is all about hanging in there, even when the going gets tough. It's that push to keep moving, no matter how steep the hill. Persevering people don't just throw in the towel. They understand that to reach that shiny goal, sometimes you've got to trudge through some mud. It's about commitment and a dash of stubbornness to not give up, even when it feels like an uphill battle.

Growth Mindset - The Game Changer:

- **Keep Growing and Glowing:** Now, here's where a growth mindset comes in. It's believing that you can always learn more, do more, and be more. This mindset is all about seeing challenges as chances to level up. Every mistake? A lesson. Every flop? A chance to grow. With a growth mindset, you're always a student, eager to learn and ready to turn 'Oops' into 'Aha!'

Put these three together, and you've got a powerhouse combo to tackle anything life throws your way. It's not just about facing challenges but using them to your advantage. Every obstacle becomes a stepping-stone to better things.

And guess what? This triumphant trio doesn't just help you; it rubs off on others too. By showing resilience, sticking to your guns, and always learning, you become a beacon for others. You're telling the world, "Hey, if I can do it, so can you!"

So let's make resilience, perseverance, and a growth mindset our go-to tools. They're the keys to not only overcoming challenges but also inspiring others along the way. Let's embrace them and make our journey one epic adventure!

SECTION FIFTEEN WRAP-UP:

Embracing and Learning from Challenges:

- Challenges shape and strengthen us.
- Celebrating successes boosts confidence and satisfaction.
- Every challenge offers valuable lessons.
- Overcoming obstacles inspires and encourages others.
- **Techniques for Navigating Obstacles:**
- Adopt a growth mindset, viewing challenges as opportunities.
- Break big challenges into manageable parts.
- Learn from experiences and failures.
- Focus on self-care and seek help when needed.
- **The Role of Resilience, Perseverance, and Growth Mindset:**
- Resilience helps in recovering from setbacks.
- Perseverance is key to enduring tough times.
- A growth mindset encourages continuous learning and adaptation.

ACTION ITEMS:

- **Celebrating Our Wins:**
- **Reflect on Achievements:** Take time to think about what you've accomplished and how you've grown from each experience.
- **Share Successes:** Inspire others by sharing your achievements and the lessons learned.
- **Set New Goals:** Use your successes as a springboard to set new, higher goals.
- **Learning from Overcoming Challenges:**
- **Journal Reflections:** Regularly write about challenges faced and how you overcame them.
- **Seek Feedback:** Ask for input from peers, mentors, or coaches on how you handled challenges.
- **Apply Lessons Learned:** Incorporate insights gained from experiences into future endeavors.
- **Navigating Life's Obstacles:**
- **Adopt a Positive Attitude:** Focus on the benefits and growth opportunities that challenges offer.
- **Seek Support:** Don't hesitate to reach out to your network for advice and support.
- **Evaluate and Adjust Strategies:** Continuously assess and adjust your strategies in handling obstacles.
- **Building Resilience and Perseverance:**
- **Develop Coping Strategies:** Find and practice effective ways to manage stress and recover from setbacks.
- **Stay Committed:** Remind yourself of your long-term goals and stay committed, even in difficult times.
- **Cultivate a Learning Mindset:** Always be open to learning and growing, despite the situation.
- **Incorporating Growth Mindset:**
- **Embrace Challenges:** View each new challenge as an opportunity to learn something new.
- **Celebrate Learning:** Acknowledge and celebrate every new skill or knowledge you acquire.

- **Encourage Others:** Share your growth mindset approach with others, motivating them to adopt a similar perspective.

CONCLUSION:

WRAPPING up our exploration of navigating life's challenges and embracing continuous self-improvement, we've uncovered a treasure trove of strategies and insights. Life's unpredictable nature throws various challenges our way, but it's our response to these challenges that defines our journey.

We've dug into the importance of recognizing and understanding the challenges we face. Whether personal setbacks, professional obstacles, or sudden life changes, acknowledging these hurdles is the first step toward overcoming them. By developing resilience, adaptability, and a strong support network, we equip ourselves to handle life's unexpected twists with grace and effectiveness.

Key takeaways include the value of a positive mindset, the power of resilience, and the essential role of a support network. Personal and professional growth, we've learned, comes from adaptability, self-reflection, and a growth mindset. These qualities transform challenges into opportunities for development, leading to transformative experiences.

Actionable steps such as regular self-reflection, emotional management strategies, building resilience, and cultivating problem-solving skills are important. We've emphasized the importance of maintaining a positive mindset, practicing gratitude, and leveraging available resources.

Looking ahead, the journey doesn't end here. The art of transforming challenges into steppingstones for success awaits, with a deep dive into the anatomy of resilience and the power of a positive mindset. We'll explore practical strategies for turning struggles into fuel for our aspirations, recognizing each challenge as an opportunity to grow stronger and wiser.

So, as we close this chapter, let's carry forward the lessons learned. Let's embrace challenges not as roadblocks but as opportunities for growth. Let's celebrate our successes, learn from our experiences, and continue on our path of self-improvement. With each step, no matter how small, we're moving closer to our ultimate goals, equipped with the knowledge and skills to turn life's challenges into our greatest victories.

ABOUT THE AUTHOR

Rae A. Stonehouse is an author, speaker, and self-publishing consultant dedicated to helping others embrace constant improvement and overcome challenges. With over 40 years of experience as a Registered Nurse in psychiatry and mental health, Rae brings a wealth of knowledge and passion for self-development to his writing and presentations.

As a 30+ year member of Toastmasters International, Rae has systematically built his communication abilities and self-confidence to share his insights as an author and speaker. His self-help books and personal development presentations aim to have conversational one-on-one connections with readers and audiences.

Rae is known for his wry sense of humor and sage advice delivered in a relatable coaching style. After four decades as a nurse, Rae has *rewired* rather than retired, actively writing and pursuing public speaking. He strives to share lessons learned to help others achieve personal and professional growth.

To learn more about Rae and his approach to constant improvement, visit his website at https://raestonehouse.com or to learn more about his publications visit https://liveforexcellence.store

∾

ALSO, BY RAE A. STONEHOUSE

VISIT HTTPS://LIVEFOREXCELLENCE.STORE/ for a selection of personal/professional self-development books by Rae A. Stonehouse.

If you have found this book to be helpful, please leave us a warm review wherever you purchased it.

www.ingramcontent.com/pod-product-compliance
Lightning Source LLC
Chambersburg PA
CBHW061136120626
46546CB00005B/1807